APPALACHIAN
REVIEW

VOL. 50, NO. 1
WINTER 2022

TRADITION. DIVERSITY. CHANGE.

ESTABLISHED IN 1973
PUBLISHED QUARTERLY
by Berea College
www.appalachianreview.net

©2021 by Berea College. Vol. 50, No. 1 Winter 2022. All rights reserved. No part of this publication may be reproduced without the prior permission of *Appalachian Review*. Periodicals postage paid at Berea, Kentucky, and at additional mailing offices. ISSN# 03632318.

CONTENTS

INTERVIEW

BOOK REVIEWS

COVER PHOTOGRAPH
Empty Bleachers by Kool Shooters

EDITOR'S NOTE

JASON KYLE HOWARD

Change: it's something we confront, and it's something we carry with us, in our pockets, inside us. Although the notion of change arguably appears to varying degrees in nearly every piece of prose, it is especially present in the fiction and creative nonfiction we have collected in this issue of *Appalachian Review*.

The theme even lends itself to the title of Gavin Colton's "Little Piles of Change," a tender short story set in Ireland with themes that reverberate throughout Appalachian culture. A working-class man is struggling to keep his family financially and emotionally afloat while navigating the changes brought about by mid-life. His wife has lost her job; his kids are growing up, their tastes evolving. Time is moving, ever so fast, and he himself feels different. How will he manage?

Christopher Labaza's "Kingsnake" shows a young man at a different kind of turning point. Pearl wants more than his meager circumstances will allow. Responsibility has come too early. He is holding his family together, while attending college and working a job that has opened him up to exploitation.

In her essay "Drought Conditions: Personal Accounts from the 2016 Gatlinburg Wildfires," Jacquelyn Scott has assembled a collage of voices that include survivors to media reports, providing an emotional, harrowing look at the tragedy and its devastating aftermath. "I will never be the same in the weirdest little ways," one survivor muses, and as the narrative unfolds, it is clear that Scott herself has been changed as well. For this is her story too—she places her own experiences in conversation with the survivors' narratives, creating a history that is at once collective and deeply personal.

For his part, Michael Dowdy refuses to shy away from the personal in "Tiny Towns," a lyric essay that takes a bracing, honest, complex look at a slice of his family's history. Through memorable imagery, language, and connections, Dowdy reaches beyond the self to link his grandfather's business of restaurants and roadside inns to *Arrested Development*, Vladimir Nabokov's *Lolita*, and the very notion of the American Dream.

Of course prose is not the only literary form found in this issue. We are proud to publish a suite of new poems from poet, translator, and teacher Jeremy Paden that will slice and heal you in equal measure. Jaycee Billington, Ace Englehart, David S. Higdon, Rebecca Lilly, Katy Luxem, and Adam Moore offer poems that reverberate with image and emotion, speaking to the senses, heart and intellect. Poetry, too, is the focus of this issue's interview. I was happy to chat with Marianne Worthington about her debut poetry collection *The Girl Singer*, which was recently spotlighted and recommended by the *New York Times*.

In closing, I want to acknowledge another change—the passing of the great critic, thinker, and writer bell hooks, whom we lost in December. bell's death is a particular blow to us at *Appalachian Review*. In addition to contributing to the magazine over the years, bell generously served as a member of our advisory board, offering expert guidance and indispensable advice even before the board was formally created. The reach of bell's work and life, of course, transcend this region and country; it's not an understatement to say that our world is much smaller, and much less thoughtful, without her. We will be paying proper tribute to bell in an upcoming issue, but in the meantime, please join us by keeping her memory alive—by being confronted, challenged, and changed by her work. ■

LITTLE PILES
OF CHANGE

GAVIN COLTON

Colly was having a pint with Pat in Kavanagh's after work. Pat had won twenty euro on a scratcher that morning and Colly knew it had been burning a hole in his pocket all day, that he'd be gunning for a pint. Colly was happy not to be going home right away.

"Nicole's back on the smokes," Colly said.

"She's not."

"She is. Since losing the job."

"Bernie said about the job, it's terrible," Pat said.

"The smoking or the job?"

"The job. The smoking too."

"It's been two weeks now. I had to tell the girls not to say anything to her. They were looking at YouTube videos and saying they were worried about their Ma because she was smoking. They think she's going to die."

"Doesn't help with those warnings on the boxes, scaring people. *Smoking Kills.*"

"And the pictures of the black lungs in the ads on the telly."

"Disgusting."

"It should be illegal."

Colly downed the end of his pint.

"Do yeh miss them yourself? The smokes?" Pat said.

"I didn't until I saw that box beside the kettle the other morning."

"I'm going out myself. Will yeh have one?"

"No. I won't. I'm grand."

Colly looked at his phone. There was a text from Nicole. He'd sent her a few job postings and a video of a granny shooting a ping-pong ball out of her arse earlier that morning that one of the lads at work had sent him. She said the furniture place in Palmerstown had called her back and asked her to come in for an interview. He wouldn't hold his breath; Nicole had the bad habit of lying on her CV, she said that employers never actually checked. She'd get away with it even if she was caught, Colly thought. Nicole was in the habit of getting away with things, and the interview would be something to get her going again, a reason to put her face on, get her confidence up.

Work at the site had been a nightmare—the concrete lads didn't show up until after lunch, so Colly and the lads made goalposts out of hard hats and one of the lads had a ball in the back of the van. Pat played in goal. World Cup singles. Colly was Luxembourg.

"Yeh can't be Luxembourg," one the younger lads off the site said. "They've never been in a World Cup."

"Neither have you, yeh scrawny prick and look at you out here celebrating like you're bleedin' Maradonna," Colly told him.

After twenty minutes, when they were all bolloxed, and the concrete lads still hadn't shown up, they left early on the promise to the foreman that they'd come in early on Monday to lay the foundation.

Pat came back from outside. The smoke smelled lovely on his clothes. "Another one?" Pat said, waving a tenner at Sinead behind the bar. She snatched it off him.

"Sinead, put two on there," Pat roared down the bar.

"I won't."

"Go on."

"Nicole will batter me."

"Sure, she's back on the smokes. She can't say anything."

Pat was right. Nicole owed him, but Colly hated thinking about their marriage like that—keeping score on each other. "Right, one more." He got comfortable again on the stool and squinted to see the telly. They were showing a repeat of the boxing from last weekend. Fury knocking the head off the Wilder fella. It was great seeing a traveler on the telly doing well, and his parents were Irish.

A group of nurses came in in their scrubs and ordered a big round. They brushed next to Colly at the bar, Irish youngones, Indian youngones, Filipinos of both genders. Fair play to them—it's hard not to like the nurses. Colly saw them protesting in town a few months ago on his way to Croke Park with the girls and Nicole. He promised a nurse fella from Nigeria that he'd vote for them when he got the chance, for the wage increase or whatever they were looking for. Colly never ended up voting, but he'd meant to and that counted for something.

Father Paul came in and took the stool at the end of the bar next to Dunny O'Leary whose girlfriend, Colly had heard, was after getting pregnant with some other fella. The rumor was that it was some youngfella that played for Bohs. Dunny looked a wreck, raking his hands through his hair. Father Paul lit a smoke and waved down to Colly; he was the only person that Kavanagh allowed to smoke inside.

Colly buried the rest of his pint, he didn't want to witness Dunny in that state. He had to get home at some point, and Pat was doing a round of shots with the nurses. He couldn't get into that. Nicole had signed him up to volunteer at the GAA disco tonight. She'd done it weeks ago, saying they needed to be more involved in the GAA club now that the girls were getting into the camogie. The proceeds were in aid of replacing the nets in the goalposts. Really, him and Nicole just didn't have the fifty euro to pay for the registration fees, a hundred euro for the both of them. They didn't have to pay if one of them volunteered at the disco. He'd been fine with it at the time, but now that the day was here, he wasn't arsed— if the girls wanted a spot on the camogie team, they could work for it themselves, washing cars or collecting cans and dropping them off down the recycling. The girls were mad into the recycling anyway, they'd love it.

Nicole had told the girls they could go along with him to the disco. They were too young to be going. Colly had protested. They were only just nine a couple of months ago. They'd had balloons at the party and one of the kids at it pissed himself. A disco was no place for them, even if it was only a fundraiser. It'd be hard enough keeping the peace between the lads who were drunk on a few drops of Linden Village without Niamh and Evelyn flying around asking the DJ to play Oasis—it was Colly's fault, blaring the *Morning Glory* album while Nicole was pregnant. When he brought the girls into town, they always joined in if a busker was singing an Oasis song. They knew some of the words to most of the songs.

"Do yeh remember the GAA disco, Pat?"

"I remember Caoimhe going. I used to be up the walls about the gear she'd be wearing. Me and Bernie nearly ended up divorcing over it."

"Over the disco?"

"The skirts."

"What was wrong with the skirts?"

"They kept getting shorter."

"Are yeh sure she wasn't just growing, Pat?"

"I didn't want that to be happening either."

It was all ahead of Colly.

"Are you allowed to kick them out?" Pat said. Colly could smell Pat, the damp and sweat from the football earlier still clinging to him.

"Who?"

"The kids at the disco."

"Why would I kick any of them out?"

"If they're drinking or fighting or getting a bit rowdy on the Cotton Eyed Joe."

"I don't think they play that one anymore, Pat."

"They should. It's a classic."

"They only listen to the lads with the tattoos on their faces and the American birds with green and purple hair, singing about stabbing their fellas."

"Bernie likes a bit of that herself. Caoimhe has her into it. That Billie Eilish one."

"Nicole likes her as well. Fair play to the girl, she gives it straight."

"She does."

"So, what'll I do if they start scrapping?"

"Tell the DJ to play a bit of Cotton Eyed Joe."

■ ■ ■

When Colly got home, Nicole was standing in the garden, smoking. She was sucking the life out it. Colly could hear the tobacco fizzing away, turning orange. When she whipped the ball of smoke into her throat, down into her lungs, he nearly felt the buzz burn through his own brain. He couldn't stand the sight of her, in front of all the neighbors, and flaunting the thing in front of him. The drink always reminded him of the taste of the tobacco, the craving in his mouth. The smell brought him back, eight years ago, before Nicole found out she was pregnant with the girls. The both of them gave them up together. It brought them closer, the pure sickness of giving them up, sweating in the bed at night and tearing the head off each other in the morning because the other one had used all the milk in the cereal. They'd promised each other that that was it. She was breaking that now. Colly hated Nicole for making him want to go back to them. He didn't but he did. He'd started to crave the nicotine again, he loved the smell of it in the house, on her clothes, in her hair, especially in the mornings with his coffee, while he listened to the news about the football, who was injured and who Eamon Dunphy thought was going to win between Liverpool and Athletico Madrid in the Champion's League.

Colly dragged the two bins up from the curb, the hollow sound of them booming up the driveway.

"Alri, love," she said. She was pure beaming under the sun, the cheek of her. "Some weather wha? I think I got burnt on my face a bit out the back. I'm getting a good base. For the holidays."

He wanted to tell her that there'd be no fucking holiday if she didn't get back working again soon. He didn't though, she'd lost her job for standing up for one the youngones in the office who'd sent a dirty pic to one of the youngfellas and now it was going around to everyone and their grannies. The lads at work had gotten it on the grapevine. It wasn't fair and there was no rule in place to punish the youngfella who she'd sent it to originally. That's how Nicole put it and Colly believed her when she came home in bits crying saying she was sorry. Nicole showed him the photo, but he felt bad looking at it, like he was spying on the poor youngone. It wasn't meant for him. Colly had heard from a woman Nicole worked with that she'd keyed the youngfella's car and he'd reported her to HR, who had it on the CCTV. Nicole had that sort of behavior in her. Colly had seen it for himself over the years.

Nicole went in for a kiss and Colly turned his cheek. She was holding the smoke out from the side of her, near Colly's face. He could grab it in his mouth. He'd eat it if he had to. The filter had a lovely pink rim on it from her lippy. It'd taste fucking lovely.

"What's up your arse?" she said.

The girls were in the bathroom. Colly could hear the radio blaring from the bottom of the stairs. The state of the place when he walked in, Nicole's make-up bag scattered on the tiles, Niamh plastering Evelyn's face in blue and red and yellow.

He needed to piss.

"What are you wearing tonight, Da?" Evelyn said. They'd barely acknowledged him. No hugs or anything. They were getting more and more independent. They didn't need him as much anymore, only for their bit of walking around money, which they seemed to need more and more of.

"I don't know, love." He nudged Evelyn off the toilet and told the two of them to get out so he could go. He'd been dying the whole way home on the bus.

"We left a couple of options out on your bed for yeh," Niamh said from the other side of the door. He zipped himself up and didn't bother with the flush.

Niamh looked like one of those youngones in Boots doing the make-up for the girls going to their debs.

"You're like Glenda Gilson," he said.

Evelyn stood on the kitchen chair they'd dragged up the stairs and was clapping her lips in the mirror on the landing, turning her face to see her reflection. Colly couldn't tell where the red ended, and the yellow began on her eyelids.

"How do I look?" Evelyn said. She was talking to him through her reflection in the mirror. He couldn't see her.

"Gorgeous, love."

"Amn't I good, Da?"

"You're fantastic. Your ma's going to kill yous for the mess."

His clothes were in three piles on the bed. Some of it, Colly hadn't thought about in years, his leather coat and his old football tops.

"Yeh have to wear the black jeans, Da."

He held them up to the light. The scissors were still there on the bed, loads of black threads around it. It looked like one of those crime scenes from the telly.

"Yous cut fuckin holes in them!" He'd bought the jeans years ago for thirty pound. They were good ones, real denim. He'd be paying over a hundred euro if he bought them today.

"It's rock and roll, Colly," Evelyn said. She picked up the scissors and started nipping at the ends of her hair with it. The damage was done.

"Rock and fuckin roll, Da."

Nicole made the three of them dinner. Beans on toast. She gave Colly a slice of cheese too. It was the last one. She was feeling bad about the smokes. Niamh and Evelyn went mad for the beans, horsing spoonfuls into them. When they finished, they stacked their plates in the sink and ran out to the road, Evelyn in her face of make-up and Niamh in her camogie kit, shin guards and all. They were already becoming different—

Evelyn was getting into the make-up and taking photos of herself on Nicole's phone, and Niamh was still trying to take her baby teeth out by eating apples. That was Colly's worry when he found out Nicole was having twins, that they'd be too much like each other and they'd never have lives of their own. They were good together though. They lived in their own world most of the time, Colly thought. They were playing invisible camogie because they'd lost their last slíothár up the GAA club watching the senior camogie women playing. They were supposed to be learning, but they spent the whole match playing out on the back pitches, while Colly stood in the rain and watched the manager Maeve Doyle roaring at the referee, calling him a culchie bastard. Colly refused to buy them another one. He put

It hurt like fuck, but they had to learn that money didn't come out of their mouths. If it did, they'd be millionaires.

his foot down, the price of the yokes. Nicole agreed with him for once that the girls needed to take better care of their things.

"It's cause we're poor that we can't have one," Evelyn had said. Colly nearly dragged her down to Elvery's Sports and dropped €12 on the counter for one of the nice O'Neill's ones, thanks very much, bud. He'd cut the thing in half and make her eat it.

He hated not being able to give them a new one, he wasn't mad on the camogie or the GAA in general, but he was happy that his girls were happy, taking lumps out each other at training. He had the €12, things weren't that bad yet, but they would be soon if he kept shelling out money every time one of the girls caught a good whack of a slíothár and sent it into the canal. He was still happy to see them improving.

"It is. Because we're poor. Your Ma and me," he told them instead. It hurt like fuck, but they had to learn that money didn't come out of their mouths. If it did, they'd be millionaires.

■ ■ ■

He was still craving a smoke. He'd love one out the front with Nicole, watching the girls whack stones against the electrical box at the end of the road while the sun set over the green. It'd be proper romantic, the two of them. He felt bad for her about the job, but he hated her more for picking up the smokes again. If he said anything, if he went mad at her, Nicole would think it was over the job, not the smokes. Colly would have only meant it about the smokes. Mostly.

When Nicole went upstairs, he thought about picking up the box there on the kitchen table. He watched it on top of the *Sunday World*, some article about a drug dealer getting shot on the north side of Dublin on the front page. The hitman was covering his face with his coat in the photo. Colly started reading the words in the article. They all fancied themselves as Americans these drug dealers, shooting each other. There was no need for that in Ireland. Colly hoped the judge would remind the hitman that he was from Finglas and not New York fuckin' City.

He shook the box of smokes. There were only a couple left. A few lonely ones. Nicole had a whole sleeve of them upstairs in the drawer with her knickers and socks, he'd seen them the other morning looking for the change for the bus. He heard Nicole barreling down the stairs again, getting ready to say something to him. He took the smokes and left out the back door and told the girls, who had climbed up a tree, to get in the car.

The GAA club car park was rammed when he got there. He walked down the line of youngfellas and youngones waiting to get in. Down by the door, Maeve was slapping her watch with her finger.

"Yeh have to check the boys' toilets for drink and drugs now do yeh hear? Every fifteen minutes," she was saying to one of the other Das.

"They're only kids, Maeve," he tried saying.

"*Every* fifteen minutes!" she repeated. She took Colly by the wrist and led him to the main door. The girls charged off out onto the pitch.

Maeve ran the show up the GAA club, hawking around the car park saying hello to the parents. She marched up and down the line of kids, all waiting in the cold to get in while Colly stood there at the door, watching all the kids in their confirmation gear and spikey haircuts clutching their fivers in sweaty little balls inside their fists. Maeve kept looking down the line to him, nodding her head and giving him a big thumbs up. The girls were running around out on the pitch with their hurleys. He could see their runners getting mucked up from here.

His phone buzzed in his pocket, next to the box with the couple of smokes.

Pat: HOW'S IT GOIN? ANY SCRAPS? HOW'S THE MUSIC?

Colly: SHITE. THE SMELL OF LYNX MAKING ME LOOPY. CAN HEAR THE MUSIC FROM OUTSIDE, SHITE.

Pat: GOOD THAT IT'S LOUD. I'LL BE DOWN SOON. WILL COME SEE YEH

Colly: DON'T COME DOWN. Colly didn't want Pat seeing him in the jeans. Colly could feel the wind against the skin on his thighs.

Pat: C U SOON.

Maeve twirled her finger in the air from the back of the line to say to open the door.

Colly let Niamh and Evelyn take the fivers from the kids. They were back and out of breath. Niamh took the money and

Evelyn gave out the change if there was any. They were making a dog's dinner of it. It didn't matter, the kids would only go and spend it on fizzy drinks and condoms from the machine in the jacks, stretching them over their heads to look like aliens. The GAA would get their money back and the girls would get their little tracksuit tops at the end of the season.

The kids smelled like Lynx and vodka.

"Thanks, sir." Colly liked that. *Sir*. The respect.

"Go on in and enjoy yourselves. No messing."

"Thanks, mister."

The hall was too big for a kids' disco, so the curtain was drawn to make it more like an actual dancefloor and less like a basketball court. Colly had fought Pat here in the charity boxing on Valentine's Day, raising money for breast cancer awareness. He could hear the shite music pumping back anytime the door opened. Once all the kids were inside, it was just the parents standing by their cars chatting the hole off each other. Colly let the girls go in after they finished counting out the money from the bag. When he recounted it, there was only €327 and a Mars bar wrapper. He did the maths in his head, there must have been at about eighty kids gone in. He looked in his wallet, he'd given the girls a fiver to split and he had a twenty he planned to use to put petrol in Nicole's car, so she didn't have to get the bus to her interview in Palmerstown the next week.

The smokers had all come out of the bar and were sending a lovely silver stream Colly's way. He pictured Nicole, at home out the front, on the phone to her sister ripping the life out of a fresh one.

The almost empty box he'd robbed off the kitchen table hung like a brick in his pocket. He took it out and shook it, popped open the tab and rubbed the gold paper between his fingers. He could smoke both of them at the same time, then never again, again.

"You can't smoke while you're working." Maeve had come out of nowhere.

"I confiscated them." She'd love that.

"From who?"

"Some boy in a red top. It's grand. Sorted. I took them off him and he was lovely about it. He even said sorry, that he was trying to quit."

"If he let you find these, think what he's really hiding! These are only a decoy."

Colly acted panicked for a second like he was considering the inner working of a fourteen-year-old druggy's head. He tried to imagine the poor youngfella, overdosed on pills, dead on the dancefloor underneath the basketball hoop with a Twix being squashed in his pocket. He could almost convince himself. The

The almost empty box he'd robbed off the kitchen table hung like a brick in his pocket. He took it out and shook it, popped open the tab and rubbed the gold paper between his fingers.

stress boiled in him a bit. Maeve was contagious. It had him wanting a smoke, getting caught like that.

"You can go inside now and keep an eye on the boys' toilets," Maeve said.

"Righ'. Grand."

"And will you tell Niamh and Evelyn to leave the DJ alone."

Maeve knew the girls' names. They'd be over the moon with that when he told them later. He'd lie too and say that Maeve saw them playing the invisible camogie and thought they had real potential, that if they kept practicing and stopped losing €12 slíothárs that they could be playing in Croke Park someday for Dublin.

It was too dark inside the disco. His eyes adjusted. He looked around at all the kids, the girls all bopping away with their arms in the air like they were taking part in some great communal drown. The lads looked worse at the dancing, like they were possessed. One girl was trying to climb tongue-first inside a youngfella's mouth. Colly knew he was supposed to break it up, hose them down. He waited to see if one of the other volunteers would go and do it, but they were all bunched together by the concession table, eating packets of crisps. He rehearsed what he was going to say on his way over. He didn't want to sound like a peado. He'd tap the boy on the shoulder and tell him that his ma was outside looking for him.

Colly was ready to go for it when he saw Pat across the dancefloor, the fat prick dancing in a ringa-ringa-rosy circle with Niamh and Evelyn. He let the youngone at the poor boy's face and bucked it over. Pat and the girls saw him coming and made some space for him in the circle.

"Howya, bud," Pat said. He had half a pint in his hand from the bar next door and was spilling it on the floor in little ruby splashes. He looked langered, big red face on him.

"What do yeh think you're up to?"

"Having a little dance with the girls. They're great dancers, aren't they?"

Colly tried to mop Pat's spills with his shoe, which only spread it. The girls were doing the leapfrog over each other and copying the older girls, trying to shake their arses.

"Yeh can't be in here dancing with the kids, Pat."

"I'm dancing with *your* kids. It's different. It's only a bit of craic."

The girls were pulling at Colly. At the holes in his jeans, ripping them into even bigger ones.

"Will yeh dance with us, Da?"

"Yeh, Da. Give us a shake."

Colly told Pat to go back into the pub. Pat skulked across the dancefloor. He was a blob of a man. The girls went after him. They'd be embarrassed to be seen with Pat in a few years. They each had a bottle of fizzy orange and Niamh had a bag of crisps hanging in her hand.

Outside the boys' toilets, Maeve had a line of lads—all in red tops—along the white wall with their pockets turned inside-out. Little piles of change, chewing, and tabs from beer cans in front of their white shoes. He wanted to rescue them from Maeve's interrogation, the poor bastards, but he decided that they probably deserved the grilling for something else they'd done or were planning on doing. They were keeping Maeve off his back.

Colly stood on the toilet seat, trying to reach the bog roll bombs that had exploded on the ceiling. Maeve would have a fit if she saw them up there, dripping on the tiles and caking into the paint. He was getting a few of them off. The ones he could reach with the toilet brush.

It took him fifteen minutes to get them all off. He was trying to get it all flushed before Maeve found him. Then someone burst in the door. Colly looked over the cubicle. It was Pat. Colly could see his sweaty bald head, he could hear Pat unzipping his trousers. Then he heard the girls with their hurleys clanging off the radiator.

"What are yeh doing up there Colly? You're missing Cotton Eyed Joe." Colly nearly slipped off the toilet seat.

"I told you to get out!" Colly said. "What are you doing?"

"Pissing."

"Why are you pissing in here?"

"The one in the pub is too busy. Half the senior hurling team is in there on the Barry White. I couldn't wait."

Pat slumped up against the urinal and started groaning when the piss finally came after about a minute of squeezing his bladder. He'd his arm stretched up the wall like he was making love to the thing.

Maeve walked in. She was raging. She might have been raging already. He couldn't blame her really. It looked bad. Criminal even.

She whispered to Colly to go home and take Pat with him. Colly hadn't expected that out of Maeve Doyle: A whisper. There was still an hour left in the disco. Pat led the girls down the hall. Colly wanted to protest, on principal. He'd been doing more than the other parents scratching their holes and robbing out of the concessions. But he stopped when she seemed to be softening in her volition. She looked exhausted.

"Sorry about all that, Maeve. I really am. I'll make it up at the next one. Promise," Colly said.

"Just pay the money like the rest of the parents and yeh don't have to volunteer. I'd rather yeh did that."

She was pushing him out the side door. Evelyn and Niamh had gone ahead with Pat, out to the car. Pat was sitting on the bonnet, showing the girls something on his phone, their faces all lit up in the dark.

Colly stopped at the table where he and the girls had been collecting the money. "Will yeh do us a favor?" he said.

"No."

"Ah please, Maeve. It's for the girls. They look up to you and didn't you only say the other week how important it was for youngones to be out playing sports, in your speech to the committee?"

"What?" She'd some frame on her. She could pick him up if she wanted to.

"That's what you said. About youngones playing sports. That it was important to invest in them because for too long, the GAA—"

"What's the favor I mean?"

"Will yeh tell the girls bye? They'll love yeh for it."

One of the volunteer mothers was running down the hall, roaring that some youngfella had climbed up the basketball hoop and got his arse stuck in the rim. Colly couldn't believe it. Maeve's face was pure panic.

"Go on, Maeve. They'll be delighted. And I'll pay my fifty euro and fuck off." "Promise?"

"Yeah. Yeah. An' anyway, I hate this volunteering shite. Sorry."

Maeve squinted over at the girls. They'd climbed on top of the car and were smacking their hurley's against each other. "Bye, girls!"

Niamh nearly fell off the car, only Evelyn caught her. They flapped their hands back at Maeve.

"Bye, Maeve."

"See ya, Doyler."

Pat joined in with the waving. "See yeh soon, Maeve, yeah?"

"No."

"Three chips and a battered sausage," Colly told Ivan, the Romanian fella behind the counter at Macaries. Ivan supported Man City, but other than that he was sound enough and always gave the girls a can of Coke to share with their chips. Pat was in the toilet again.

Colly couldn't go home yet. Nicole would be asking questions and the girls would grass him up. They wouldn't mean to, but they would. Anyway, the girls would be delighted with the few chips and hearing what Maeve Doyle had to say about all the potential they had.

"Eleven euro," Ivan said. Colly gave him the twenty out of his wallet and Ivan handed back the change and a can of Coke for the girls. Nicole could get the bus, she deserved to.

Colly stuffed the change in his pocket, in with the two lonely smokes rattling around in their box. The holes had gotten bigger over the course of the evening. The pockets were now on the outside of his jeans. His good black jeans. Like dog's ears. Ivan had a tip jar with a Man City crest on it on top of the glass counter that displayed the menu. He'd told Colly weeks ago that he was saving up to go over to the Etihad for a match. He said he wanted to bring his new fella with him too as a surprise. His new fella was from Roscommon, Colly had only met him the once in the pub and he seemed sound enough. Colly would never have guessed it on his own.

On the day of the referendum, while he was picking up the dinner, Colly told Ivan that he'd voted YES and so had Nicole. He wanted Ivan to know where he stood. They liked supporting all the new shite coming into Ireland, the gay marriage, the immigrants coming in and making the Irish better looking, saying fuck off to the Catholic church. Colly remembered one journalist, the McWilliams fella, saying that Colly's generation were the Pope's Children. It's good

It's good for the country to be changing, moving forward, as long as they don't lose the bouncy castles at the Communions, that's sacred stuff.

for the country to be changing, moving forward, as long as they didn't lose the bouncy castles at the Communions, that's sacred stuff.

But Colly couldn't support Ivan's trip to the Etihad, that would be criminal. He liked leaving the odd tip for Ivan, even if it wasn't much, he'd see Ivan outside the pub smoking. Ivan had bought him a pint once and Colly had never bought him one back, he still thought about that when he saw him sometimes. He dropped the two smokes into the jar instead of the change. Man City had just gotten banned from the

Champion's League that week and fined some mad amount of money. Surely tickets would be the bit cheaper now there was no European football on the club's horizon.

"Salt an' vinegar?"

"Loads of it."

Ivan handed Colly the bags of food.

"Thanks, Ivan. Sound."

"Cheers, boss." Colly loved when Ivan called him boss in his big Romanian accent.

The girls passed the can of Coke between them, then to Pat, while they milled into their chips, coughing into the bag when the bang of vinegar hit their throats.

"Did I tell yous, girls? What Maeve said about yous?"

"What?"

"Wha?"

"Yeah, wha?" Pat had his hand in the girls' chips. Colly was saving the last bag for Nicole. She'd be out the front when they got home. He'd give her a kiss, a nice long one, bit of tongue if she was having it, just to taste the nicotine. That would be enough for him to get him through the night. Until the next morning and the craving was back in his bones.

"She said yous have real potential. In the camogie. Saw yous swinging at each other on top of the car. She knows talent when she sees it."

The girls went on scoffing the chips, ignoring him.

"What do yous think of that? Exciting, isn't it?"

The two from the disco walked into the chipper, who'd been eating the face of each other. He was glad he let them at it now. Young love.

"Well?" he said to the girls.

"The thing is, Da," Evelyn started. She looked at Niamh, who was shaking her head at her sister. "We don't like camogie anymore." Niamh buried her head in the chips.

All the make-up had run down Evelyn's face. She looked like a gone-off banana, all yellow and purple.

"Yous only started a few weeks ago. I just bought yous new hurleys and the helmets and all."

"There's too much running, Da," Evelyn said. "Isn't there, Niamh?"

"You never get the ball," Niamh said. Colly could tell that this was Evelyn's doing. She'd convinced Niamh to agree with her.

"I can't believe this," Colly said. "The money me and your ma spent. Yous aren't quitting."

"We can sell the gear at the book fair at school," Evelyn said.

"Yeh can't sell hurley helmets at the book fair. Yeh can only sell books."

"Not true, Da," Niamh said. "They sell maps of Ireland, pencils, 3D glasses, an' DVDs."

"Yous aren't quitters. I won't have it. Yous can't just be hanging around the house in the evenings watching the telly and annoying me and your Ma." He was raging inside. He'd spent over a hundred euro on helmets and hurleys and a few slíothárs for them. He'd had to save up. Colly took a big breath and relaxed his shoulders. He let all the tension out of his face. It was something he'd started doing, for his anger. Breathing.

"See it out until the end of the season and if yous still don't want to play then I won't make yous."

"What's wrong with quitting?" Pat said.

"Don't get involved, you," Colly said.

"They'll find something else to do, wont yous, girls?"

"We want to dance instead," Evelyn said. Niamh was nodding her head again, in agreement this time.

"Dance classes? Like ballet?" That sounded expensive to Colly.

"There you go. Yous are great little dancers," Pat said.

"Not classes, Da. We'll go into town and dance while the people are singing and put out our own guitar case to get our own money. Won't we Niamh?"

"The guitar case has to be red on the inside!" Pat said.

"Where will you get a guitar case from?" Colly said.

"The book fair!"

"Yous will make more money if it's red," Pat said. He was emptying the dregs of the chip bag into his mouth.

Colly regretted throwing the smokes into Ivan's jar now. He felt suddenly sorry for Man City (and Ivan), losing all that money and the Champion's League ban. Poor Maeve back at the GAA club giving up her Friday night. The youngone from Nicole's work, her face and them some plastered on phone screens everywhere.

He'd think more on it in bed later. He didn't like the idea of them quitting anything. It was a bad habit to get into young. Colly's parents had never let him quit anything, even after he came home from the boxing with a broken nose two days before his confirmation. His Da looked upon it as a badge of honor for the family, and his Ma waited until the swelling and the bruising went down a few weeks later to do the photographs.

Nicole was watching telly in the kitchen when they got home. She'd the backdoor open and was having a smoke. It was always cold in their kitchen, especially on the tiles. They'd no underfloor heating like some of the kitchens Colly installed. The breeze brushed in against his face. He glared at Nicole, sitting there with her legs tucked under her arse. He didn't know how she could still be so flexible at her age, but she was. He felt the muscles in his jaw grab onto the bones. The girls were straight up on her. He gave her the chips. She tore open the bag on the table and started picking at them with her spare hand.

"How was it?" she said. No thanks from her.

"It was grand," Colly said.

"They played Oasis."

"Maeve Doyle kicked us out!"

"She what?"

"Shut up, Evelyn!" Niamh said.

"Listen to your sister," Colly said. "It was grand, it was good craic actually." He was looking at Nicole now, trying to convince her. He took a handful of chips and told the girls to up and wash their faces before bed. Nicole had just lit the cigarette. There was loads left on it. She offered it out to Colly, then took it back, and hid it under the chair.

"I don't want to tempt yeh, I'm sorry."

"I know, love. It's grand."

"Here." She stubbed the smoke in the ashtray, then shook the tray over the sink and rinsed it out. The telly was playing one of the shows where people buy themselves a second house in Lanzarote. It showed a long, sweeping shot of the sea view from villa's master bedroom.

"That'd be nice, wouldn't it?" Colly said.

"One day," Nicole said. She sounded so sure saying it.

He went into the sitting room to watch something else. He waited for Nicole. He wanted her to come sit with him. He wanted to talk to her about the interview, about giving up the smokes. He promised himself he wouldn't go mad at her. A while later, he saw the lights go off in the kitchen and the sitting room door pop open. He pretended to be asleep so Nicole would wake him up. She was so gentle rocking his chest with her hand.

"Will we go up? I'm knackered," she said.

"I'll be up after you." Colly turned off the telly—he hadn't really been watching it. He folded the girls' blanket and fixed the pillows on the sofa. One of the girls' shoes was on the ground, he didn't know whose it was, so he kicked it under the sofa where they could find it when they needed it.

Nicole was peeping into the girls' room when he made it up the stairs. He stood behind her and put his hand around her, under her top. He made a little circle around her belly button without going into it. He didn't want to tell Nicole about the girls quitting the camogie. He could convince them to keep it up. He'd find a way to do it. He didn't care about the money, but he cared about the quitting, the giving up. Their little bodies bobbed on the beds. He felt Nicole's breathing go a bit shallow. He swallowed the air in his mouth, he was preparing to say something. He didn't know what yet, but Nicole stopped him by putting her hand over his mouth. He let his lips fall open and stay on her palm. It was enough. He was glad she hadn't let him say anything to ruin the moment, watching the girls sleep, his breath warming against her skin. ∎

'ATA 1966

After eight days adrift in the South Pacific,
the six boys found themselves marooned on an island.
This is not what you think. None was named Piggy.
Not one of them wallowed in that muck and mire
that men from cities think to be the state
of humans in the wild. They used their spears to fish
and not for war. Once they lit their fire,
they worked in shifts, two by two, to tend it.
They raised a garden, found a way to save the rain.
When one fell off a cliff, they clambered down
to bring him up, then made a cast of leaves to set
his broken leg. Can we not sing them instead?
Sing how boys will come together, how they'll work,
how they'll make guitars of coconuts and driftwood,
and greet the dawn and dusk with song and prayer.

JEREMY PADEN

SWIMMING

I stood beside the ambulance still swimming
through the grey Michigan waves. When the cop
asked for my info, I mumbled an address
one address ago, stopped, corrected myself;
then flustered and breathless gave my wife's number,
a number I'd thought forgotten now that all
I do is press her name when I want to call.
Midway through, I stopped again and gave him mine.

He looked at me and asked, You sure? Yes, I said.
And tried to catch my breath, to reel my mind
back in, mind that still swam toward the man, worried
we'd both drown, that still went over those lessons
in that Caribbean cove where I would swim
past the breakers, then dive down to touch bottom,
where dad would have us swim up behind him
and drag him back to shore through choppy surf.

When the ambulance left, I sat on the beach
and watched the horizon, still swimming. That night,
I chopped and sautéed onions for dinner,
all the while swimming, swimming to reach him.
His absent eyes bobbed just above the water.
I slid my arm under his pit, across
his chest, his body rested on my hips.
The waves washed over us. They pulled us down.

A limp man weighs much more than a father
trying to teach his son to save a life.
I left him on the shore, left him to the care
of others and then collapsed. He called after

dinner to talk. His wife and her sisters
had gone to town to shop, while the guys
and kids had gone to swim one last time,
one last swim before the end of vacation.

Two days later, back at home, he called again
to tell me once more all he knew; to ask,
again, what I had done. Unable to free
himself from the undertow, his mind still trapped
in a body that couldn't touch bottom.
All he remembered was mumbling a prayer
and giving up. How, when he had a wife
and daughter, could he have fought so little?

He said he saw Jesus swimming to him
through the waves and then, spent, he passed out.
How did I reach him when his wife's brothers
could not? Days later and he was still caught.
I told him of when a car ran a light,
broadsided me, crushed my ribs, bruised my brain.
How months later at stoplights a glint of sun
off windows in my peripheral vision

would make me cry, strip all strength from my legs,
so they could not accelerate the car,
told him how the headaches and short temper
lasted for years, how only recently
I had begun to venture again into the sun
without glasses. But there I was, on the shore
of Lake Michigan playing with my children,
catching waves whipped up by some western storm.

My wreck and my survival was dumb chance.
That he and I were at that beach, coincidence.

Life is a matter of fractions, accidents.
It was luck that knew how to swim through surf,
luck that pulled a drowning man back to shore.
We want the intervention to be more;
we want God, but get tired, troubled angels
swimming to reach us through the cold, grey waves.

JEREMY PADEN

ON MIGRATIONS

a pair of kites, of Mississippi Kites,
birds that live in Entre Ríos, Argentina
from the end of August to the end of April
& that in Spanish are called *milanos boreales*,
or northern kites, nest & breed in the woods
of the park near our house, & have for at least
four years now, they come for the cicadas
& dragonflies & the long days of sun,
the ornithologists at www.audubon.org
say they're gregarious, that they migrate
in flocks & nest in loose colonies, the map
they include does not identify central Kentucky
as a nesting site, & truth be told, one pair
does not a colony make—throughout the south
there are towns like Carthage, Mississippi,
connected for over twenty years now
to Comitancillo, Guatemala,
a few came for jobs & went back home,
then returned with cousins & friends
& everyone in that Guatemalan city
now knows someone in the north & a small
dying town in the south now bustles again
with children & cookouts & people who love
that flat red earth & the slow Pearl River—
in the history of the great 20th century
migrations, not the ones that families
like Ilan Stavans's made fleeing pogroms,
Jews almost never returned, but those
of Italians, Greeks, Germans, who starving
& huddled came chasing a dream,
not caring enough to distinguish between

the shores of the River Plate or the Hudson,
note that high percentages returned home,
some who came back to try again & others
who, like crazy uncles, went home to never
leave the house again—I wonder Luis, is
this pair of birds an adventuresome vanguard,
pioneers of a new colony, that first Juan
& María that settled & made a home
warm & wide enough to harbor new wanderers
who roam the world in search of an honest wage

JEREMY PADEN

BLACK HOLE SUN

excellent, let's talk about the stars, Luis,
let's talk about lights & their satellites
way up in the sky, & let's talk about your name
that comes from luster, from something bathed
in light, like the moon or like a clear night
dressed up in a petticoat of spikenard
oh satellite, satellite of love, there,
high in the night sky, colored like a plum—
we walked out with naked feet on the frosty
ground of the garden at 4 in the morning
to watch the moon, as that shadow passed, blush
from a solar hug, thank you for the metaphor,
the early hour brought to mind when my wife
& kids & a friend of our daughter & I
left Lexington before sunrise to arrive
in Hopkinsville just after first light
because on that 21st of August, minutes
after midday, a *pas de deux* was to begin
that would culminate at 1:24 pm
with a sun completely darkened by a 3
minute kiss, like that long, slow kiss
between Ingrid Bergman & Cary Grant
in *Notorious* that mocked the Hays Codes—
hundreds of us had gathered in the field
& all of us were left breathless, my parents,
who had driven 10 hours to be with us,
responded to that sacred spectacle
by singing psalms once they had their voice—yes,
of course, these are utterly natural forces,
this attraction that keeps star & satellite,
planet & moon in orbit, that work to line up

these 3 enormous bodies, they are undeniably
common, everyday & outright holy—I remained
silent, agape, to quote your namesake
(that gardener & school teacher Ludwig
Wittgenstein), when faced with what we
cannot name, silence...

                                eclipses
have their fan clubs, their *Dead Heads,*
who go from show to show chasing
the high, & I wonder, how many faithful
will have congregated today, December 4,
in the Antarctic, how many pilgrims
will have made the journey to witness the kiss,
that moment when the moon dresses up
in the *ring of fire* of that *black hole sun*

JEREMY PADEN

FROM *HOW TO RECOGNIZE GOD'S CHOSEN*

xxxviii.

the faithful will come to zhe
& demand a song of zion,
so zhe will turn & chant:

praise the sturgeon & the lungfish
praise the ginkos & echidnas
the puzzle monkey tree & the horseshoe crab

but zhe, the faithful will say, we want
a song of heaven, of everlasting life,
so zhe will turn again & sing:

praise the resurrection plant & lichen
the snapping turtle & the hellbender
praise the yew, the bristlecone pine, & the sacred fig

but zhe, sing to us of a time outside time,
they will say, sing to us of the great beyond,
so zhe will turn & lift up with hir voice:

praise the work of roots, rhizomes, & mycelium
praise, praise the eastern juniper & shaggy-maned moss
the ant, praise the ant & bloodroot & trout lilies & wild ginger, praise

DROUGHT CONDITIONS:
PERSONAL ACCOUNTS FROM THE 2016 GATLINBURG WILDFIRES

JACQUELYN SCOTT

WBIR-TV

November 1, 2016—Because of the danger of wildfire, the Great Smoky Mountains National Park has temporarily banned all backcountry fires.

East Tennessee is in the midst of a drought, and with the falling leaves now on the ground, the danger of wildfire is very high. Thousands of acres have burned across the state in the last few weeks because of the extremely dry conditions, and last weekend, the U.S. Forest Service implemented strict fire restrictions in the Cherokee National Forest which limits fires in undeveloped areas.

'With the current drought conditions, it is imperative that we reduce the risk of human-caused wildfires during this period of extreme fire danger,' said Superintendent Cassius Cash. 'The park has not banned back country campfires since 2007, but these unusually dry conditions warrant the restriction.'"

Me

I am twelve. I am standing in the middle of the Whaley-Big Greenbriar Cemetery in the Great Smoky Mountains National Park, looking down at the headstones, thinking about my relatives beneath me. I have followed my mother and grandfather on the trail that leads to the cemetery, pausing on the bridge to take pictures. They are talking now, and I wander off. Most of the headstones are small—little arch-shaped rocks placed in the ground with initials and two dates carved lightly on the face, like someone had engraved the stone with the tip of a knife. I want to find the largest headstone, the one that is prettier than the rest, the one that signifies that person had been the best of them, or at least to me. I find her in the far-left corner. Her headstone is white, with cherubs carved on either side. I can't read her name, but I can make out enough of the years to understand that she was a baby when she died. Did she die from something we can cure now? My mother calls for me. As I'm walking back down the trail to the car, I stop at the ruins of an old school. I wonder: if my great-great-great grandparents weren't forced out to build the park, if that school still stood, if my family never migrated down from the mountains, would I be the same person I am now?

Anita

"My dad was a pilot, so we moved around a lot." Her voice over the phone is a steady stream of courage in my ears. I listen and hope the recorder is picking up her words. She lived in Gatlinburg for twenty years off and on but moved there permanently after her divorce in 2012. "I was trying to find out what life was like on my own." She describes her life on top of that mountain as a fairytale. She uses words like *beautiful, peaceful, empowering.*

Mary Ann

"I've lived here all my life." We're sitting on her swimming pool deck facing the road, and cars often drive past. Sometimes, she lifts her hand and waves, and I don't know if she recognizes the people or if she's just being friendly. She used to ride her bicycle on these roads during a time before there was traffic, before there were tourists. I assume she is older than she looks, at least fifty or sixty. She says she used to garden and raise her chickens and swim in the river. "The happy things," she calls them.

Scott

We sit in his camper at his small dining room table. If we stood side by side and stretched out our arms, we could probably reach the front and back together. The remains of his burned house sit just outside the door, and before I knocked, the harsh reverb of aluminum resounding through the trees below, I stood at the very edge of his charred and broken driveway that is cut into the side of his mountain, and I looked down at the crowns pointing up at me. What would it feel like, I wondered, to have everything I've known or loved burn up all around me?

Rikki

We sit on a couch in the middle of her studio apartment that overlooks the mountains. Reverent, I think. I would love to live in this place. She says it still feels like a hotel. Her hair is growing back in as tight black curls. I tell her how pretty it is, and she pulls on one and lets it bounce back up. She shaved it about a year ago because her lupus made her hair fall out in clumps, leaving her with little bald patches all over her scalp. When she talks, she seems much older than she is; I have to remind myself she is only twenty-three. She paints her fingernails a pretty dark grey as we speak, and one of her tattoos peeks out from underneath her sleeve. I can't see all of it, but I know it says, "Fear no love." I have a similar one painted across my ribs: "Fear no evil." Sitting with her brings back memories of a time when I was twenty-one. She was the first I told about my cervical cancer. She was the one who talked to me about hardship and loss. What could I say to her that she doesn't already know?

■ ■ ■

Knoxville Daily Sun
"November 23, 2016—The Chimney Tops 2 Fire reported in Great Smoky Mountains National Park near Gatlinburg, TN on Wednesday, November 23, 2016 at approximately 5:20 p.m. The wildfire began burning in a remote location (Chimney Tops) of the park in steep terrain with vertical cliffs and narrow rocky ridges making access to the wildfire area difficult for firefighting efforts."

■ ■ ■

Me
I follow my father as we hike the two miles on West Prong Trail into primitive campsite eighteen. He's carrying our tent in his hands, the rest of his gear packed in his backpack. I'm

carrying our food—chicken and sandwiches. We get to the campsite and pick a spot next to the creek. He sets up the tent while I hunt wood for a fire. The land is greener than anything I had ever seen. I am thankful for the national park, for the ability to escape into the wilds of my mountains and live for a night the way my relatives might have before they built their cabins.

Our neighbors, two young men, are looking for dry wood on the ground, but I found it all first. Maybe there is something in my blood, some ability passed down through generations that helps me in our mountains. In the morning, I stir the ashes, looking for hot coals. When I see some, glowing red from the night before, I throw dry leaves in and blow little puffs of air until the fire kicks back up. The young men aren't awake yet. We eat s'mores for breakfast and leave before they rise.

Anita

I close my eyes as she speaks and try to picture her life. Coffee on the porch with her two dogs. Standing up and taking off on a walk through the woods behind her house. What would it be like to live so close to the wild?

Mary Ann

She cries often, and I am helpless watching. What could I possibly say to make it better?

Scott

He tells me about the free counseling the Helen Ross McNabb Center offered to people who suffered through the fires and says it was one of the best things that ever happened to him. Before, he couldn't sleep without the help of alcohol. "I had it figured out that if I did six shots of whiskey and a half-hour *Seinfeld* episode and drank a beer, I could go to sleep." Therapy is not a sign of weakness, he assures me. It's a sign of strength, and I agree.

Rikki

When I ask her to describe her life before the fires, the first words she chooses are "oblivious" and "naïve." I had never thought of her this way. She then laughs and says, "Indestructible. I'm Super Woman." And this is more like the Rikki I know. A pillar of strength.

Me

I spend many nights at the bar across the street from work. My best friends and I open the doors and walk in, greeting the bartenders by name. We sit in a line on our stools in our black tank tops—our Buffalo Wild Wings jerseys lay crumpled in the back seats of our cars—and wait for the rest of the crew to show up. I go outside often and look up at the mountains in front of me, wishing I could be there instead.

Anita

"I'm sure you'll hear this word again." Fireballs. "The wind blew fireballs through the air, and when the wind died down, the fireballs would drop. Whatever they landed on would burst into flames because it was so dry." So dry, people were losing their wells. She had dirt coming out of her faucet because her aquafer was so low. What would happen if all the water ran out, I ask? She says, "I don't know."

Mary Ann

There was only one way out. A fireman yelled for them to go and not stop. "The smoke was so thick, the winds were so high, the flames were shooting over the vehicles, and we couldn't see the road." She wondered, how could anybody who didn't know the way make it off the mountains? I say, "I don't know."

Scott

He was in the kitchen making something to eat, and he turned to look out the window. "What do I do, I thought? What do I do? The whole sky was like a scarlet red I've never seen." As he was looking for his fourth-grade daughter's cats all over the house, his deck caught on fire. On his way down the mountain, he called his ex-wife and said, "If I don't make it out of this, tell the kids I love them."

Rikki

She tells me about little things she lost—her makeup, a card she received from her great aunt when she was nine, a necklace of her father's ashes—and I consider what things of mine I would lose, what things of mine I would miss. She says that everyone keeps telling her that it's her life that matters. She looks at me and says, "I'm not any less grateful that I'm alive, but I would like to have these things as well." And, I think, I would too. Some things can't be replaced.

■ ■ ■

Gatlinburg Daily Post

"November 29, 2016—The wildfires severely impacted our beautiful national park and the northern gateway communities of Gatlinburg, Pigeon Forge, and Wears Valley last night. While information is still being gathered in the light of day, we know that tremendous destruction has occurred.

Hundreds of acres within the park have burned, including areas of Chimney Tops, Mount LeConte, Bullhead Trail, and Roaring Fork Motor Nature Trail.

As of this morning, Great Smoky Mountain National Park officials have closed all facilities in the park due to the extensive fire activity and downed trees. Great Smoky Mountain Area operations at our Sevier County, TN, visitor center locations, our headquarters near Sugarlands, and our mail order department are also closed at this time.

We are also saddened to report that many long-time friends of Great Smoky Mountain Area, including local businesses that support us and this park, have lost their homes and businesses. Our thoughts and prayers are with them."

■ ■ ■

Me

I sit in my Chattanooga townhouse 153 miles away as my mountains burn. I watch, powerless, as people post pictures and videos of their homes and land, destroyed. I text my family and friends. What can I do, I ask? What do you need? They all reply, *everything.*

Anita

"In all of the ways. In all of the ways I was affected. But I made it out with my life and my pets and my blender." She tells me she doesn't want to say Divine Intervention, because that means God had her back but not her neighbor's down the hill.

Mary Ann

Her son had just been named as The City of Gatlinburg's Fire Marshal and Arson Investigator. "It was tormenting knowing he was up in the mountains fighting that ungodly fire." She spent the next few days after the fires waiting to get a phone call that he was dead.

Scott

"Those little girls who burned, they went to school with my daughter."

Rikki

She describes what she remembers as a horror movie that was the night of the fire. She says her house was burning while she was still inside, her eyes tearing from the smoke. The traffic was backed up in the road and trees were falling everywhere. She had to park her car and run in between the traffic, and as she was running down the road, a bear ran off her mountain and crossed in front of her. "I sounded like I was hyperventilating from the smoke in my lungs, and I had pocket-dialed my best friend in my purse. She was on the phone thinking she was listening to me die."

Me

I walk down the Ramsey Cascades trail with my husband. We want to camp, but the creek is too high to cross. I lead him back down and take him to my cemetery. It's been so long—over thirteen years—that I'm not sure I remember the way, but I find it. I pretend it's because I have a magnetic pull to my great-great-great grandparents, and some place deep in my heart wishes it was true. We walk around and look at the headstones. I show him the baby's grave with the cherubs. It doesn't seem so large to me anymore.

Anita

She didn't think her house was going to burn. She thought she could wait it out and drive back home in the morning. "When I first knew things were bad, I was talking to a sheriff's deputy. I asked him how long he thought it would be before I could get back up to my house, and I told him where I lived.

He said, 'Ma'am, if you've got someplace to go, I suggest you get there.'"

Mary Ann

She received phone calls from ADT intermittently alerting her to different areas of her house catching fire. Every couple of minutes she answered the phone and listened: her garage, her kitchen, her living room, her bedroom.

Scott

"Everything is based around tourism here in Gatlinburg. So, at first, the city officials thought it would be in bad taste to build a memorial for those people that died." I can't imagine their deaths going unnoticed. Ignoring the lives of fourteen souls?

Rikki

I ask her if she went to see her house as soon as the mountains were opened to the public. She laughs and tells me the only thing she thinks about when she remembers that day is that she had just shaved her head because of her lupus, and a woman yelled to her through her car window and called her "sir." Then she says that because has she lived here all her life, she knew a back road she could use when public safety had everything else blocked off. "It was *Dawn of the Dead* with no one around and all the destruction."

Me

I gather everything I can think of and divide it into bags to give to my friends. Some stuff I don't use anymore, some I do. Clothes, shampoo, soap.

Anita

"I used to wonder what they do when the cameras go away. Those people you see on TV standing in front of the rubble of their homes after a fire." But now she knows. They go to Walmart and buy a toothbrush. "There were seven of us lined up in our pajamas looking at the travel sizes." They didn't speak, just looked at each other.

Mary Ann

She told me her son said she didn't understand. He was twenty-five feet away from a lady he couldn't save. He told me he watched her burn, she said.

Scott

"My daughter blamed me for her cats dying. She blamed me for her friends dying. She didn't talk to me for almost eight months." As he talks about how difficult it is to be apart from her, I think about my dad and remember a time as a teenager when I didn't talk to my father either. I want to reassure him in some way that maybe when she gets older, she won't blame him anymore. She won't see him as the villain she has made him out to be. But every situation is not the same. I say nothing.

Rikki

"You could tell where everybody's bedrooms were because of the bedsprings."

USA Today

"November 30, 2016—Though officials have confirmed seven deaths as of Wednesday, many are worried about additional fatalities because several people still are missing. Debris and downed power lines have limited authorities' abilities to explore.

Among the missing are a 61-year-old Memphis couple, Jon and Janet Summers, who were separated from their three sons as they tried to escape the wildfire early Tuesday. The young men were found injured, transported to a Nashville hospital burn unit and are in critical but stable condition.

Portions of Sevier County, where Gatlinburg and nearby Pigeon Forge are located, received about a half inch of rain overnight Tuesday and are expected to get an additional inch or so Wednesday.

While the wet weather helps firefighters, the rain likely won't penetrate the piles of dry leaves and brush that have accumulated in the forest through the years, according to Gatlinburg Fire Chief Greg Miller."

■ ■ ■

Me

I am in the backseat taking videos with my phone. My father drives us around the back roads, showing us where the fires started. We trace our way from mountain to mountain, following the path the flames took. Even now, two years later, there are distinct lines of char and ash where the fire scorched its way through the trees.

A respite from the tragedy, we drive through Cades Cove and stop to look at the cabins. We walk inside a few of them, trying to understand what life might have been like. It's cold outside, and air flows through cracks in the floor. I close my eyes and try to imagine what it would have been like to suffer through the winters in those cabins, building fires in the large hearth that would warm the entire room. How would they have slept on those nights with ice puffing up from below, the flames licking warmth on their cheeks? Did they huddle together on the floor trying to trap the warmth between them, taking turns to wake and check if the embers hadn't creeped too far from the fireplace, then stoke the flames to keep them going? If the fire had gotten out of control, what then? Where would they go?

Anita

It was the first time in her life where she really felt alone.

Mary Ann

"It was like driving through a warzone," she says, describing her visit back to her house after the fires. She only went back once.

Scott

He tells me when he was finally allowed back up to see his house all he found were cement blocks, and I ask him what that was like. He doesn't answer me at first, glancing instead out his solitary window to the mountains that surround us.

"It was like a shot in the heart."

Rikki

She laughs often and breaks her poignant stories with lighter comments. We stand at her window while she points to different ridges. "Sometimes I use binoculars to see what other people are doing." She picks them up as if to demonstrate. She offers them to me, and I take them in my hands, lift them to my eyes. I look out her window with them, just to see.

■ ■ ■

The Daily Times

"December 7, 2016—Two juveniles are being held in the Sevier County Juvenile Detention Center on charges of aggravated arson in connection with the Chimney Tops 2 fire that left 14 people dead, scores injured, and more than 1,700 structures destroyed or damaged.

The juveniles face aggravated arson charges in the fire in the Chimney Tops area of Great Smoky Mountains National

Park on Nov. 23. Amid hurricane-force winds, the fire spread to the Gatlinburg area early last week, causing widespread damage.

'Our promise is that we will do every effort to help bring closure to those who have lost so much,' said Tennessee Bureau of Investigation Director Mark Gwyn.

The juveniles are from Tennessee, but not Sevier County, where the fires spread. Otherwise, officials said state law prevents releasing more information about them. The investigation is ongoing and more charges could come, and Dunn said it was possible the case could be transferred to an adult criminal court."

■ ■ ■

Me

I am standing on the landing of the new Chimney Tops Trail. We can no longer go all the way to the top. I look out over the mountains to the scorched, black-tipped rocks. They look like real chimney tops now. Let's go see the gate, my father suggests. We turn, walk down the trail, but stop—there's a bear, digging in the ground, blocking our path. She pauses and looks at us. I take pictures. She's so skinny. Too skinny for it to be August. She trails us up the path, no doubt smelling the banana and bagel in my husband's pack. We hurry up a small side trail to hide and wait, hoping she doesn't follow.

Anita

"My closest neighbor in proximity, his wife left and went to Kroger and couldn't make it back up the mountain. He went to leave, and I saw his taillights going down the road." She thought they made it out, but he got blocked and had to come back up. "He perished in that fire, and his wife had just gone to the store."

Mary Ann

She thinks the fires divided the town. "Everybody wanted to blame somebody, and I have my own opinions." She wants to know: how could it be that those boys got off without having to pay a price of any kind?

Scott

"I lost everything." His three-bedroom house, his daughter's pets, custody of his daughter. He didn't have insurance, so he is unable to rebuild. Instead, he used the money from the Dolly Parton Fund to buy his small camper.

Rikki

"I just didn't want to be alone."

■ ■ ■

Knoxville News Sentinel

"December 28, 2016—A month after the Gatlinburg wildfire on Nov. 28, a look at the numbers:

14: Deaths attributed to the fire, 12 directly from the fire, one by suspected heart attack, one who sustained a medical event and died in vehicular accident while fleeing fire

191: People treated at hospitals for fire-related injuries, illnesses

2,460: Number of structures damaged or destroyed in the fire

17,904: Number of acres burned. 17,140 in the Chimney Tops No. 2 fire, 764 in the Cobbly Nob fire

80: Number of firefighters from 40 states and the District of Columbia during the peak suppression activity".

■■■

Me
I sit across each person and repeat, repeat, repeat myself. How long have you lived in Gatlinburg? What did your life look like before the fires? What does your life look like now?

Anita
"I will never be the same in the weirdest little ways." Now, she keeps a pair of shoes by her bed, a sweatshirt hanging by her door, her purse in the same spot every night. Her car always has gas in it, her cell phone is always charged.

Mary Ann
"We have simplified our lives." She tells me that when people go through something like that, they learn to live without as much stuff. It's relationships that matter.

Scott
"From what I heard they're saying all the Gatlinburg fires were started by downed powerlines. That's disheartening. To think that somehow the fires those kids started at the Chimney Tops four or five days before our houses burnt down didn't have some type of correlation, to me that's insanity."

Rikki
"I thought I was going to die that night. There's no other way to put it. I mean, how do you fight a forest fire? I was twenty-two. I had no idea I should leave my house. I didn't think it was a possibility my house would burn down. That kind of thing has never happened in a place like this."

USA Today

"June 30, 2017—Prosecutors have dropped charges against two Tennessee teenagers they labeled as responsible for the state's deadliest wildfire in a century, an attorney confirmed Friday.

Defense attorney Gregory P. Isaacs said the state can't prove that the horseplay of the boys, ages 17 and 15, that sparked a fire in the Great Smoky Mountains National Park caused the deadly wildfires in Gatlinburg, Tenn., five days later.

The boys were hiking on the Chimney Tops trail in the Great Smoky Mountains National Park on Nov. 23 and tossing lit matches onto the ground around the trail. Brush caught fire. The boys continued hiking down the trail. A fellow hiker with a Go-Pro happened to catch footage of them with smoke in the background.

Park officials decided to let the fire burn. Five days later, winds of nearly 90 mph whipped up, spreading deadly flames into Gatlinburg and Pigeon Forge. The emergency response was fretted with flaws, including the failure to warn residents and delayed evacuations."

■ ■ ■

Me

I haven't seen my mountains for months, but I'll be back. I always go back.

Anita

"Before, it was take-your-breath-away beautiful, and it delighted my soul. But after the fires, it was so ugly." It was not the fairytale she loved anymore, and she wasn't sure if she was going to rebuild. "I couldn't find any houses anywhere else I looked, and I thought that maybe, the reason I couldn't find anything was because I had already found the perfect place."

Mary Ann

"It's one of those things in life that changes you, that makes you appreciate life more." When she thinks back on the fires, she thinks about how God helped her get through. She says He helped her get down the mountain, He helped her when she could not see.

Scott

We talk about a bear that crawled in his Jeep. He shows me pictures of the paw prints in his seats. I tell him about the skinny bear I saw on the Chimney Tops Trail and the bear looking for food in my mom's backyard over an hour away by car. He says their food supply since the fires is scarce. I ask him if he thinks the park should plant the trees and bushes that were lost. He says they don't have the budget for that kind of thing. How much more damage can humans cause before the world crumbles around us?

Rikki

She went to Helen Ross McNabb for therapy, and while she was sitting in the waiting room, the staff yelled back and forth to argue if they were still taking fire victims because it had been six months since the fires. Even if it had been six months, even if it had been five years, you still have a right to talk about it, I tell her. She says she feels like a ball of emotions, with her compounding anxiety, anger, and depression. "My boyfriend tries to get me to go talk to somebody, but it sucks, you know. Because I tried to go talk to somebody, but I just ended up with that terrible experience." I want to reach for her, to take her hand and say, "You can talk to me." But I don't because the recorder is still on. When I leave, though, I hug her and tell her she can call me anytime, already knowing she won't. I will text her soon, I think. But until then, I hope I have done enough.

■ ■ ■

WBIR-TV

"November 28, 2017—On the one year anniversary of the Gatlinburg and Sevier County wildfires, a permanent memorial for the victims and first responders was announced Tuesday at the 'Day of Remembrance' ceremony.

The bridge crosses the river near the Gatlinburg-Pigeon Forge city line, and a trail will go from downtown to Herbert Holt Park.

Officials said they hope to begin construction in the next three to four months, and city leaders say the end result will honor the lives lost for generations to come.

City and county officials also took time at the memorial service to remember the lives lost in the fires and honor the first responders and volunteers for their service in the days and months that followed.

Hundreds of people filled the gym at Rocky Top Sports World for the service. It's a place that only one year ago was filled with more than 2,000 people in need of shelter after evacuating from the fires.

The service included a moment of silence for each of the 14 lives lost in the fires, remembering a tragic part of the past in a city forever changed one November night one year ago.

Wilson said, 'There will always be that one thing that we were all a part of that we wish never happened, but I can say this, I believe the city to me looks more beautiful today than it ever has.'"

Me

Five years later and the Chimney Tops still bear the marks of that day. The rocks remain scorched and frail, the surrounding trees remain dead. I can still follow the fire's path by the charred trees through the mountains, and there are still lots that remain empty, now barren concrete slabs where a home used to stand. But it is not all devastation. There is new vegetation where ash used to be. Chalets, churches, and restaurants are restored, and tourists once again fill the streets. It is almost as if the fires never happened, if you don't look too closely. But for those of us who bore witness and have been unable to rebuild, it will forever live in our memory. ■

NEPTUNIAN PRECAMBRIC

It doesn't take much for me to slip out of myself, like a fish, to shapeshift into astral excrescences, a Neptunian Precambrian imaginal. A hint of the tragic and I'm out. In diffuse light, in seaweed crumbling on rock, I gulp water and salt as my fins flop while my poorly-de-signed gills work hard to extract minute amounts of oxygen. I've never transcended myself in my poems, but live in false oblivion. You'll have to swim out, as I did, to find a poem of your own, holding your breath, diving from your lifeboat. If you're mindful enough, the joy is immediate and close.

REBECCA LILLY

KINGDOM OF THE MOON

Uncle Walter, dishonorably discharged
from the army, built me a fort at the top of
a rambling oak—a sturdy treehouse for a
twelve-year old. As if I were a banished
queen, I'd look out with binoculars,
searching for red ants in armies, and
whittle swords out of limbs within reach.
Your silent enemies besiege you, Walter
shouted, but you're a whipper-snapper on
the kingdom of the moon! Now in middle
age, I laugh him off, but remember Walter
as a little scary. I'm still nostalgic about
the woods where I walk, classifying herbs,
plucking moss sprigs and lichen. My
family cemetery overlooks the whole
range of sparsely populated trees (the
forest clear cut for houses) where for
hours I've searched the rubble of graves,
cross-examined myself obsessively, and
on some days, fallen in a chasm, a thin
sallow moon with bluish craters, a catch-
all for my inspiration. The scenery gets
 abstracted and vague as if wind breathed
in mist and shadows grew the darkness
where I memorized epitaphs, to honor
sovereign moments I hold in common
with the dead.

Long ago, I lost my passion for analysis,
for charting out shadowlands with exact
coordinates. Now I catch voices in the

psalms, fluttering pulses from some extraordinarily clear summit. When the moon touches flowers I left on sunken stones, one sparkle's enough: a floating ember of rock dust, but like a blossom's cup, spiked in panicles, both deep and delicate.

REBECCA LILLY

MARIANNE WORTHINGTON

As a child growing up in Knoxville, Tennessee, in the 1950s and 1960s, Marianne Worthington was surrounded and subsumed by country music. Her parents often tuned their television set to WATE, the local station that aired Knoxville businessman-turned-mayor Cas Walker's *Farm and Home Hour* variety show, which featured established and rising stars including The Everly Brothers, Chet Atkins, Roy Acuff,

Carl Smith, Bill Monroe, and perhaps most famously, a talented young girl from Locust Ridge in neighboring Sevier County. Dolly Parton captivated the young Worthington, whose keen musical and poetic ear was already being tuned to a special kind of frequency: the particular blend of power and vulnerability woven into Parton's songs and those of other female country singers including Loretta Lynn, Patsy Cline, Jeannie Seely, and later, Emmylou Harris.

Worthington's debut poetry collection *The Girl Singer*, published in November by Fireside Industries, an imprint of the University Press of Kentucky, pays tribute to these women and others like them, and to the beloved women in her own family. In voices that croon and praise, rage and lament, Worthington has created a moving history that is at once collective and personal. In a recent interview with *Appalachian Review* editor Jason Kyle Howard, she spoke about the threads of country music, feminism, grief, and nature in her life and work. The interview has been lightly edited for clarity.

■ ■ ■

JKH: Three main themes tie this collection together: grief, nature and country music. How and why are these themes connected for you?

MW: Honestly, as I was struggling to put the manuscript together, I wasn't sure that these themes *were* connected. Luckily, I had readers and an editor who helped me see they were connected by pointing out how the themes showed up in my work. I could see recurring emphases and emblems, and the poems began to organize themselves around those themes. Outside of the book, grief and nature have been my

Marianne Worthington　　　　　*photo: Dereck Hammers*

companions since February 2020. (Isn't that true for so many of us?) And country music was constantly in my head, like a lullaby, since I was an infant and well up into the late 1980s, anyway.

JKH: Country music history is so deeply woven into many of these poems, and into your own life as well. Many of the artists that appear in the book predate your lived experience of consuming the genre. Have you always been someone who has studied country music and its history?

MW: Yes, I've always been interested in the music, stories, and histories of county music. As a kid, I listened to country music because that's what my parents listened to, and they knew a lot about country music performers, which I picked up just by listening to them talk. Living in Knoxville, my parents had attended the live radio show *The Mid-Day Merry-Go-Round.* My Mother told me she had seen Maybelle Carter and her daughters at a show. My parents kept up with which musicians were in town for performances. Audiences like my parents had this type of respect, related to pride of place especially, for East Tennesseans who were famous in country music: Chet Akins, Roy Acuff, Carl Smith, Homer & Jethro, Brownie McGhee, and of course, Dolly Parton. My parents loved music and they both were very good singers. In college and graduate school I began to read and study music in a more formal fashion, and I had teachers who encouraged me to write about music.

JKH: What is the history of the term "girl singer"? While you nod in the book to its pejorative roots, you also seem to be trying to reclaim and repurpose the phrase as one of empowerment.

MW: I'm not sure I can relate a history outside of how I know the term to be used; but basically, starting with early barn dance radio, men were always the headliners in country music shows. Women performers would be invited to share the stage with them as their "girl singers." In the 1960s and 1970s Loretta Lynn was The Wilburn Brothers's "girl singer." Dolly Parton was Porter Wagoner's "girl singer." "Girl singer" implied a type of ownership, really, as well as an obvious subservience to male performers. Women performers have always understood the label of "girl singer," and many have fought and are fighting to overcome its connotations. I hope the poems draw attention to rescuing and reclaiming the phrase as one of power.

JKH: A lot of Appalachian women of your mother's generation may not have used the word *feminist* to describe themselves, yet they are remembered as such strong women. Would you call this book an intentional act of feminism?

MW: Absolutely, yes. I get so aggravated about how the term "feminism" has become this loaded, ugly word in our language now. Many people, men and women, only see stereotypes when faced with the term. And while there is no one definition of "feminism," I like to define it as the opportunity for equal self-expression. My grandmothers were without husbands and never remarried. They were very self-sufficient and steady role models of how to be both a working parent and head of the household. Many women performers had this same determination and strength. I saw it in my own family and playing out in front of me on television when I watched women singers in country music. I wanted some of these poems to honor that tenacity for self-expression.

JKH: Who are some of your favorite female country singers? Why do they and their music resonate so deeply with you?

MW: Well, Dolly, of course, because she's been with me since I was a tiny child. Also, though not country singers, I loved gospel singers like Vestal Goodman and Dottie Rambo. I idolized Mahalia Jackson, whose records I listened to at a cousin's house. Her voice was so *big*, and I loved how she broke all the rules of singing, like breathing in the middle of a word. And, truth be told, I was also mesmerized by Jackson's long-time piano player, Mildred Falls. But really, Emmylou Harris is my very favorite, and not just because of her voice but because she has taught me so much about the history of American music through her recordings. With every album, she honored past musical traditions and stepped forward with new musical innovations. I remember being in the car with my father when we heard her for the first time on the radio singing "If I Could Only Win Your Love." My father asked, "Who is that singing that old Louvin Brothers song?" And I said, "Who are the Louvin Brothers?" So from the beginning, I had to go find out about Ira and Charlie Louvin as a way to better appreciate what Emmylou was doing in 1975. I wanted to write my master's thesis on Emmylou Harris but my advisor wouldn't get on board. I still adore Emmylou.

JKH: Some male country singers—Marty Stuart, for example—show up in the book as well. Why did you decide to include them?

MW: Because like Emmylou Harris, Marty Stuart honors the roots of American and country music. And the poem "I Saw Bobby Bare Kiss Marty Stuart" is a true story and was such a riveting experience that I wanted to write about it as well as try to figure out why I cried through most of that long concert.

JKH: One of the more powerful elements of the collection is how realistically and movingly you examine grief. It's deeply resonant, but it's never sentimentalized—yet in writing, reading, revising and re-reading these poems, you are to some degree reliving the illnesses and deaths of your parents. Has that been mostly difficult or healing for you?

MW: Mostly more difficult than healing, I think. I'm glad I could get the poems down—and some of them I drafted in hospitals and nursing homes—but you never stop reliving the illnesses and deaths of your parents. So writing the poems hasn't been healing, per se, but more like helping me come to some kind of closure. It's really difficult to write about your beloved dead people and animals without becoming a slobbering fool. I always have to check my tendencies toward sentimentality.

JKH: You write about the natural world with such appreciation and with a keen eye, and I can't help but wonder how that is connected to your identity as a poet. Would you say that you are an observer of the natural world because you're a poet, or would you be more likely to say that you're a poet because of being an observer of the natural world?

MW: I am no good at riddles! I wouldn't say that I had an "appreciation" of nature as a child, but I was outside all the time as a kid. As long as we came home before dark and my parents had a general idea of where my sister and I were, we roamed the neighborhoods freely. My family and their friends made many picnics and day trips to Norris Lake and other lakes nearby. My mother's people still lived on a farm that we visited several times a year. We lived at the base of the Great Smoky Mountains National Park. I saw so many bears when I was a kid and waded in many a cold creek in the Smokies. I went to camp every summer. So, I learned a lot about nature by being out in it, and that really never left me.

JKH: You're a poet who likes to use different literary forms on the page. Sonnets, pantoums, and newer, more experimental forms. What's the most challenging poetic form for you to write and why?

MW: The contrapuntal (or hinged) poem with two voices, like the poem "A.P. Carter v. Sara Carter," is quite challenging because the two voices together also have to make a third voice. It's like working a puzzle. It's fun, but it is hard to get it right. I love knowing about forms and patterns and reading poems written in form. Poetic forms can be good templates for ironing out your thoughts or for motivating you to write by trying your content out in a particular form. It's especially fun to break the form/pattern and play around with inventing new "rules" for the form. I admire seeing and learning about new forms. When I was writing "Roll Call" I made up a pattern I wanted to follow: three line-stanzas of eight syllables each and each line ending in the same sound. I wanted that pattern to do the work of describing a particular bird. At first it was just a way to get me started, but I ended up keeping the poems in that shape because they were so much fun to write and I hoped that joy would somehow be conveyed in the form.

JKH: Are you able to pick a poem in the book that you could say you're most proud of having written?

MW: That's a hard one. I am pretty happy with the way "On Seeing a Letter Patsy Cline Wrote to Nudie the Tailor" turned out. Originally, the poem included parts of the actual letter Cline had written to the famous rodeo tailor about making her some new clothes. But when it came time to publish the poem in the collection, I could not get permission to use the words of the actual letter from the owner of the letter (despite some really good help from people in Nashville). So I had to take the poem apart and rewrite it. I didn't think I could do it, and I was ready to just scrap the poem and leave it out of the collection. But then after a good little meltdown, I got to it, and I'm okay with how the poem evolved.

JKH: As we know, the publishing world—and the world-at-large—all too often devalues and ignores women once they exceed a certain age. *The Girl Singer* is your debut collection, and it's been released to much buzz and acclaim, even getting a high-profile write-up in the *New York Times*. Now that the poems are out in the world, how are you feeling?

MW: Old. And happy. And amazed. ■

I LIKE TO WALK
BEFORE THE LIGHT

I like to walk before the light,
before life unfolds, where no things

stir except in dreams and dark
is mine to wander.

Days like that I can render fat
from fallen leaves and holt,

and finally breathe, let wild thoughts
leave me, sinking into water.

Left of me is this—

the sky, a deathbed blue, blankets
the black-toothed sentry,

and feral things, wilder than I,
break limbs under hoof and crown,

and deadened leaves white as pearl
defy mirrors of still water,

till dark drops and colors rise—
first ochre and oakmoss, then flames

tip the tops of the eldest trees,
and fog melts my ocean pasture.

DAVID S. HIGDON

EASTERN CEMETERY

Etruscans built graves from bedrock clay,
away from the living,
outside the city.
Cemeteries carved with gabled roofs,
doors & windows framed from stone.

There were patio tombs,
porches to commune
with neighboring shadows and wraiths
emerging from a terminal mouth
like Leviathan devouring its hosts.

But not all graves garnered great rooms,
bodies stacked,
forty thousand, then fifty.
Love on top of love on top of
plastic flowers—unraveled, rusted, & bent.

There were great piles of dirt,
shovelfuls on top of shovelfuls.
Mounds compensate for settling.
The coffins, charred & deckled,
collapsed, a depression left in its wake.

DAVID S. HIGDON

THE LAMP ABOVE MY DOOR

is where I watch buck
moths and mayflies cling
the gentle strobing, wings
drumming against the fragrant
oilskin of night sky—drawn
like sentinels to the mine,
flutters and twitches and drops
in their cages.

The lamp above my door
is my heart's conflicted beacon,
wayward sibling of the Furies,
born of seafoam, terns
bolt from foghorns steering
toward a rock-jagged shore.
I am wrapped in ruin, retrace
pathways to thorn-filled nests
full of birdsong.

DAVID S. HIGDON

KINGSNAKE

CHRISTOPHER LABAZA

He walked along the weed-stubbled shoulder of the road, carrying a paper sack with two cans of sweet corn and a dead rat. His shoulders were slumped in towards his chest, and moonlight fell on the budding hunch of his back. Though the sun had long retired behind the white pines, the heat had yet to dissipate, making his hairline and armpits damp with sweat.

This was summertime, when the air stayed hot all night, like a simmering broth of molten lead, any breeze nothing more than a ladle that stirred the heat around. This was Georgia.

He was still wearing his tan visor and apron, with its little plastic name badge that read *Wade's Good Friend* EARL. His name wasn't really Earl. But Wade—of Wade's Food and Grocery, a short balding white guy in his late fifties who wore oversized knock-off Jordans—had misheard him when he'd said, "Pearl." That, or he wanted to keep the "P" their little secret.

Pearl didn't bother to look as he crossed the quiet street, knowing nobody would be out this late. Nonetheless, he half-jogged across the asphalt until he reached the weedy gravel of the roadside. A little farther down, he turned left at the stoplight that blinked hypnotically above the empty intersection.

The thick rubber soles of his shoes found the sidewalk and dragged against the coarse concrete. His legs were sore but remained locked in perpetual motion after his double shift. Working fifteen-and-a-half hours wasn't strictly legal, but there wasn't much *strictly legal* about Wade.

"If you make me happy, I'll be good to you, boy," he had said, a certain look in his eye, when he handed over the freshly-made name badge.

"Yessir," was all Pearl could reply.

Now, after three months of working at the store, Pearl realized that Wade always had some certain look in his eye—a spark of giddy, puerile delight that time had not wiped from his aging face.

Pearl's pace quickened as he turned once more, this time into his apartment complex. Even in daylight it didn't look much like a "complex": just a small cluster of shabby, single-story units built around an amorphous stretch of unmarked pavement that was both road and parking lot. His was the fourth door down in Building 5C, the one farthest from the road, sunken back into the surrounding woods.

On his doorstep, he removed his visor and apron, neatly wrapping them together and tying it with the apron's cord. He dug into his pocket for his keychain. There were no lights, but his fingers easily found the keyhole and the door clicked open.

Inside, Pearl stepped out of his shoes and crept through the dark, aware of the sound of his breath brushing through his cracked lips and the squish of his sweat-soaked socks on the vinyl floor. The place was small and the walls were thin, too thin for the discordant sleep schedules of his family. There was also a chance that his mother was still awake, but encountering her this late never led to anything good. When he reached the kitchen, he slowly uncrinkled the top of his paper bag, pulled out the two cans of corn—careful to avoid the rat—and left them on the table. One can had a few dents in its side, but free food was free food.

"You're a skinny little shrimp, aren't you," Wade had observed one day while Pearl loaded boxes of chicken nuggets into the freezers. Startled, Pearl turned to see his boss leaning against the glass a few doors down. His eyes watched Pearl's body as it worked.

Before Pearl could respond, Wade continued, "If you're hungry, you should eat." He gestured to the frozen pizzas with a grin, winked, and left.

Since then, Pearl no longer had to pinch dimes from his mother to pay for groceries. Even when she had been working three jobs, there never seemed to be quite enough money for food but always enough for beer. He didn't take much from the store, and what he did take was either expired, rotting, or damaged goods, but so far it had been enough.

He crept over to the couch, a few feet away, eying the lump of blankets under which his little brother slept. Squinting,

he searched in the darkness, the only light the green glow
of the microwave clock, until he saw his school-issued iPad
tucked under the five-year-old's arm. With a sigh, he reached
down and lifted the boy's wrist carefully, holding it by the
tips of his fingers so as not to wake him, and slipped the
tablet out from his brother's grasp. As he turned to go, his toe
struck something soft. Peering down, he saw that it was Mr.
Buttercup, Jamie's old teddy bear. Pearl picked it up and placed
it in the empty cradle of the boy's arm.

When he reached his room, he took out his keychain
once more and unlocked the door. He flipped on the light,
temporarily blinding himself for a second, and then checked
to make sure everything was the way he'd left it: his twin bed,
sheets tangled, twisted, and draped on the floor; crumpled
cans of Red Bull, assorted clothes, and flattened cardboard
scattered here and there; a broken, long-forgotten pull-up bar
in the corner. Relieved, he set the iPad down and hurried to
the large tank on his little desk.

"Hey, Vanilla Bean," Pearl whispered, tapping the glass
with his fingernail. "I brought you a little snack." There was
a slight rustling of shredded newspaper. A tiny white and
black-speckled head appeared, its two tiny eyes mesmerized
by the movement of Pearl's bony finger. Without looking away,
he reached into the paper once more, this time pulling out
the dead rat by the tail. He dangled it in the air, and the snake
flicked its tongue.

"Look, buddy," he said, lowering it into the tank. The rat
was dried out and odorless after being out in the sun all day,
but Pearl hoped there'd still be some meat on it.

He had found it in a little nook by the dumpsters where
some of his coworkers liked to smoke. Not a smoker himself,
Pearl had hoped for some relief from Wade's gaze for a few
minutes while he ate dinner. He sat on the curb, eating, and

watched the sun turn the sky pink and gold. But halfway through his bologna sandwich, the bald man's puffy head appeared around the corner.

"Thought you could escape me, did you?" Wade said as he trotted over. "Here." He held out a cigarette.

Pearl feebly took the gift and stared at Wade's feet. His shoes were two sizes too big, he noticed. Wade was wearing two pairs of socks. Pearl looked past the faded red and off-white sneakers, and that's when he spotted the rat, laying in the small slit between the dumpster and the brick wall of the store.

Wade stepped closer, shooting jets of smoke from his nose towards Pearl's face. Pearl knew better than to wince or cough.

Suddenly he was standing over Pearl, towering above him despite Wade's usual short stature. His fingers were brushing through Pearl's blonde hair.

"I like you, kid," Wade said with a sigh. Pearl looked up. The dying sunlight gave the man's bright red face an eerie glow, casting harsh shadows on his round features. "Even if you are a little scrawny and pale. You could lose the piercings, too."

Wade paused, looking Pearl over. "Not perfect, but I like you."

Wade was slowly closing the distance between them. His cigarette fell from his hairy fingers and he laid his sneaker over it.

Suddenly he was standing over Pearl, towering above him despite Wade's usual short stature. His fingers were brushing through Pearl's blonde hair.

Pearl's body tensed. He tried to swallow. The smell of Axe Body Spray and tobacco seeped into his nose. He didn't move. He couldn't breathe.

■ ■ ■

Vanilla Bean slithered out from under the newspaper to examine the rat as Pearl lowered it into the tank. Pearl smiled as he watched the curious little head bob up and down, the beady eyes sparkling and the tiny tongue flicking out from under the frumpy nose. Two black splotches on top of his head almost looked like a little hat. Vanilla Bean's long, speckled body shimmered in the dim light. When he reached the carcass, he turned back again and dove beneath the newspaper shreds, as if repulsed by the offering. But Pearl knew he'd eat it eventually.

Although California kingsnakes were usually fast eaters, Vanilla Bean was not. Even as a hatchling, the snake had always taken food reluctantly. Pearl and his cousin Chloe— who'd secretly given him the snake in the first place—used to drop frozen pinky mice into opposite ends of the little snake's tub and watch intently as the snake took its time considering both, laughing with glee when he finally ate one or the other. That was a long time ago, before Chloe and her parents stopped coming around, cut off contact completely, finally took that job offer on to the West Coast and moved away—all on account of Pearl's mother.

"You're going, just like that?" Pearl had heard his mother say from his room. "You're leaving me and our home?"

"The truth is, we've put up with you long enough," his aunt said. "You know, this place might be bearable if it wasn't for people like you."

"You mean people like us."

"No, people like you."

"I'm your sister, bitch!"

"Are you?" His aunt paused, then yelled, "Chloe, say goodbye, we're leaving."

A few weeks after they'd gone, Pearl found his mother on the porch.

"Can we go to California, too?" he had asked.

"Oh, Pearly. You know we can't do that," she'd said, sipping something dark and strong.

"Just to visit?"

"There's no leaving this place, Pearly."

"Please."

"What did I just say?"

That was a long time ago, and things hadn't changed.

Now Vanilla Bean was fully grown. He was Pearl's pride and joy, and his big secret. Neither Jamie nor their mother had ever seen the snake, and Pearl always locked his door to keep it that way. If his mother ever found it, found out where he'd gotten it, she'd surely lose it, drunk or not. And that would be the end of it: Vanilla Bean and a lot more. And if he told his brother, Jamie'd tell their mother.

Pearl stood and wiped his hand on the seat of his pants. He emptied his pockets, dropping his driver's license, the cigarette, and a wad of cash onto the desk. He eyed the money, hesitant to touch it but eager to call it his. He hadn't looked at it for more than a second when he'd first found it in his break room locker earlier that night. He knew what it was, what it was for. And if it hadn't been clear enough, someone had written "HUSH HUSH" across the face of the first bill with a fat black Sharpie.

Pearl picked up the wad and slowly leafed through it, laying each bill on the desk and counting as he went. There was $70 in all; the bills were still crisp. He looked down at the money for a minute, losing himself in the richness of the patterns and linework, the variety in fonts and scripts, the subtleties in shades and color—so many details he had never really considered. Money usually left his hand as soon as he got it. But looming over the intricate designs were those thick

82

dark words "HUSH HUSH," a black stain. The handwriting reminded Pearl of the blocky way Jamie wrote his name.

He sighed and collected the money into a single stack. There was a slight, pleasant heft to it. Reaching behind the snake tank, Pearl pulled out a small tin box covered in stickers of dolphins in sunglasses and dogs under beach umbrellas.

It was empty except for a short message written on a sticky note that had lost its stickiness:

Hey Pearl!

I miss you!!! I ask my mom every day if you and VB can visit, and she said she'll think about it! I'm so excited! You will love it here. Our house is right next to the beach! I picked some seashells for you. Hopefully see you soon!!!

Your Cousin,
Chloe

Pearl read the note over a few times and couldn't help but smile. He had no idea where the seashells were now, or where Chloe was now, for that matter. Still, he couldn't help but smile, which soon faded.

"Why do you want to leave me?" Pearl's mother had said when he'd told her about the note—leaving out the part about the snake. "And our beautiful trees? The mountains? Why do you want to leave us?" She had been sitting outside in a plastic chair, talking to someone on the phone. She gestured to the mountains, barely visible over the roofs of the apartments and the gas station sign across the street. But there they were, the blue ridges poking out above the lush green treetops. Maybe his mother was right: they were beautiful, in a way.

He folded the stack of bills in half and put it into the box, secured the lid, and tucked the box back behind Vanilla Bean's enclosure. The snake followed the motion with his head, then settled back down into the newspaper shreddings.

"What do you think, little buddy?" said Pearl. "Do you think old Wade has more than fives and tens in his wallet?"

The snake stared blankly back at his owner, unblinking, unmoving.

"You're right," Pearl said. "Let's not talk about that stuff." He shook his head, trying to clear his thoughts. An icy chill ran down his back, and his breath drew shallow.

He checked the time on the iPad. It was just past three. He unlocked the tablet, closed the game Jamie had fallen asleep playing, and checked the notifications. There was a new message from Professor Keeley, the woman who taught online Graphic Design classes at the technical college nearby. Pearl only took one class at a time, but he was hoping to eventually get a degree in web site design.

The cold water on his skin reminded him of the way the beads of sweat had dribbled off Wade's hand and run down his spine, leaching into his flesh.

REMINDER: Assignment #4C is DUE on Friday, June 12th @ Midnight.

He sighed and rubbed his eyes. It could wait.

Leaving his room, he tip-toed to the bathroom, where he pissed and undressed. He ran cold water from the faucet and used a rag and the bar of soap to wash himself at the sink, showers being too loud at this hour. He started with his bleach-singed hair and scrubbed all the way down to his feet, trying to get rid of the dirt and the sweat, the smell of Wade's Food and Grocery. The smell of Wade himself.

The cold water on his skin reminded him of the way the beads of sweat had dribbled off Wade's hand and run down his spine, leaching into his flesh. He had done his best to control his breathing, to remain still.

"Relax," said Wade from behind him, massaging Pearl's neck and shoulders with his meaty palms. Pearl opened his mouth to protest but nothing came out. Wade stretched out Pearl's collar, digging down past the lean muscles into bone.

But before Wade went any further, an eighteen-wheeler rumbled around the side of the building. Wade instantly drew back and walked away as if nothing had happened at all, waving to the driver as she went by. Once she began to back into the loading dock, Wade turned to Pearl and flashed his signature smile, then disappeared.

Pearl sat in a daze for a few minutes, unable to think or move. He heard the truck's engine die and the voices of the driver and one of his coworkers, but he couldn't tell what they were saying. Everything was faint and blurry, the shapes of the building and the dumpsters and trees oozing into the bloody purple of the sky. After one last, deep breath, Pearl stood, leaving his half-eaten sandwich on the curb, and began to walk back inside. He moved shakily at first, doing his best to compose himself. Pulled his shoulders back, held his head high, and mustered his dignity.

He'd gone back later for the rat.

■ ■ ■

After drying off with a hand towel, Pearl slipped into pajama bottoms, double-knotting the drawstring. He returned to his room and dropped his dirty clothes into a pile on the floor. He looked into the tank, but Vanilla Bean still hadn't eaten. Pearl shook his head.

"Come here, you," he said. He reached into the tank and rustled through the shavings of newsprint until he found his scaly friend. "Let's get you out of there."

The snake wriggled as Pearl lifted him out of the enclosure but then relaxed into Pearl's grip, wrapping around his wrist.

Moving to the bed, Pearl switched off the light. He lay down on his back and set Vanilla Bean down on his bare belly. "Roam free, little guy."

The snake took a moment to untangle itself, then slithered across Pearl's skin, exploring the plane of his abdomen. When he approached an edge, Pearl instinctively lifted a hand to corral the snake back towards the center of his body.

He closed his eyes and let his chest rise and fall with ease, feeling the motion of the snake like one long muscle across his stomach. Pearl's flesh tingled slightly as the scales passed over it, soft and cool and fluid.

His mind wandered. He imagined the ocean, deep and blue, waves gently crashing in tune with the rhythm of his lungs. He could almost smell the salt and hear the seagulls. There were surfers relaxing on the beach and sailboats gliding across the water. A light breeze across his face, swishing through palm trees. Cloudless skies. The warm glow of the pleasant San Diego sun.

Light chatter on the boardwalk, the sound of running feet, and, what was that? Laughter? Yes, laughter. A group of guys, kids his age, were coming up the walk. Tossing a ball between them. Smiling. Gym sharks. Rainbow swimsuits. Muscles.

He felt Vanilla Bean bump into his waistband, and he lost his concentration. The scene started to fade. Faded to black.

Out of the darkness, the face of Wade appeared. Wade at home, asleep beside his wife. He was a snorer. She was hogging all the blankets. A dog—a German Shepherd?—was curled up at the foot of their bed.

Down the hallway to the individual bedrooms of Wade's children. Pearl knew their faces because sometimes they came by the store at the end of Wade's shift. Now they slept in their beds. Peacefully.

Pearl could tell they were Wade's family because they all had that little smile on their faces, that glimmer behind their eyelids. They slept peacefully.

It was clear, in Pearl's mind at least, that they didn't know the whole picture of what went on at Wade's Food and Grocery. How Wade marked his money.

Pearl felt a slight twitch in his cheek.

What would Wade's wife do if she knew? Leave Wade? Kill him? Kill Pearl?

Pearl's face was getting warmer.

No matter what, something had to end.

His heart beat faster.

What was he complicit in? Any of it? All of it? He saw Wade's face, an indiscernible, ever-changing expression: delight, shock, anger, pain. *She's left Wade.*

Pearl no longer controlled the cadence of his breathing.

Delight. Shock. Anger. Pain. *She's killed Wade.*

He squeezed his eyes tighter, trying to go back to the beach. He wanted the sea. But all he saw was Wade.

Delight.

Shock.

Anger.

Death.

She's killed Pearl.

Vanilla Bean was writhing around on Pearl's chest, his collarbone, his throat.

Pearl grabbed the snake right below the head. He whipped it into the air, and it thrashed back and forth, flailing at both ends. But it couldn't escape Pearl's grip.

Pearl fought to keep himself from clamping his fist shut. The snake was strong, but he knew he was stronger. Strong enough.

A sharp sting shot through his hand. His fist shot open, and Vanilla Bean fell to the floor. He almost yelped out in pain, but he caught himself, glancing sharply at the door. He jumped out of bed and hurried to the light switch, clanking through the cans on the floor.

His eyes watered at the sudden burst of light; he let the tears fall.

When his vision cleared, he was peering down at a red ring on the back of his hand. He knew the bite wasn't venomous, but it still hurt. It hurt to move his fingers.

Pearl wrapped his hand in a shirt and searched for Vanilla Bean.

"I'm sorry, buddy," he said, "I wasn't thinking." He repeated this over and over. "I wasn't thinking. I wasn't thinking." To the snake, to himself, to the empty room.

■ ■ ■

By the time he found Vanilla Bean, coiled in the back corner of his closet, his shirt was soaked through and heavy with blood.

"You got me good," he said. "But I deserved it. Sorry." He held out his clean hand and waited, waited for a long time, for the snake to come to him.

Returning Vanilla Bean to his tank, Pearl noticed the dead rat on the shredded newspaper. He sighed. He knew that it would be eaten by morning. Knew that the bleeding should stop soon, that his hand would be fine. And he knew that Wade's money could save them all. ■

SOMETHING IN THE WATER

"As much as she loved Waycross, she hated cancer more."
                    —*Joshua Sharp,* Atlanta Magazine

The collection tins ring
        passed around numb
                like communion to toss

dirty change into:
        fundraisers for
                the many afflicted

families after prayers
        run dry. The kids'
                faces are flyers glued

around steel cans
        sitting on store counters,
                nailed to light poles,

faces missing from class,
        from church. And it's the kids,
                the poor kids, or the old

folks, the poor ones,
        who've worked the yard,
                or live nearby. In the trailer

parks by the tracks, there's not
        a single family without
                cancer. Squatting gallon

tumors with no preventative
     care; deep medical
          burdens that drain

the whole community,
     the list of sick toddlers
          rattle longer and

longer, fever-bright.
     Canals ooze from superfund
          clusters; blister folks

remember the Brunel Street
     canal catching on fire.
          Mast ships would dock

in the St. Marys for the black
     water once. Now people
          are scared to eat its fish.

Over steeped dark ditchwater
     tea where the runoff from
          the railyard seeped and crept.

JAYCEE BILLINGTON

MOUNTAIN OF NIGHTMARES

1. Crest

I cannot stop thinking about dead lesbians.

Four months after our first camping trip,
a few days off and miles away from home,
the *dura mater* reminds me: how their camp was found
one half of a mile away from their car, parked at Skyland Lodge.

Stop thinking about Skyland Lodge,
elbow-deep in the Shenandoah hills of Virginia
where the ticket booth opened into a fork
where I sat in a sticky leather seat in the middle of a bus,
chaperoning a youth camping trip back in 2017
when I still wore my hair long and my nails painted,
where I left our sleeping kids under the careful watch
of our Army-vet turned Teen Director
as I walked past the amphitheater & across the road

from our campsite at Big Meadows—
the same grounds Lollie and Julie had camped in 1996—
where I stood beside a dumpster, under a lamppost,
my back to the wind as I phoned the boyfriend back home
who had insisted I call more out of jealousy than concern &
where, in the morning I toasted blueberry muffins over fire,
filled each little hand before we cleaned up camp,
left no trace, and drove home.

2. Summit

I recognize that this is not the same
place or time that I previously existed,
not the mountain on which I first called
to a god, my father's god—
these are mountains whose secrets
lay clotted on earth floor like *arachnoid mater*—
the village I was raised by, traded
for one that will not stop looking at us
when we hold hands.

A failure against a predator puts a definite end to reproductive potentials of prey animals

In an interview, her friend says:
She just wanted to live in a world that was not hostile.

The young woman had been found murdered, along
with her partner in the Shenandoah Valley.

And this isn't the first time—not even along this Trail—
we have been killed for a kiss.

It becomes habit to look for the signs that remind me:
you are here.

But a hunting failure is merely a missed meal for a predator, not precluding further breeding.

Our biggest fear that day, hiking the Upper Higgins:
trying to cross the stream without slipping
or dropping the camera while our ten-year-
old dog trotted back and forth,
up and down, watching after us
and I wonder if their dog, Taj,
had seen his mothers' souls as
they lifted through the
forest trees.

Her father was the one who notified police they were missing;
   telling reporters that focusing on their lesbian love is distasteful—
   takes away from a brutal murder—though if, in fact, they were intimate,
      he would support whatever made her happy.

3. Descent

She is worried I'm not sleeping:
   it's the similarities though,
I tell her so she understands—
      how we, too, wandered not far from the car,
      how even our names sound similar—
   but I know she understands
   because we made it out and kept going.

She asks me if I am still sure I want to do this—
we aren't married yet and she understands if I would rather
run off with a man—she knows I haven't been down these roads.
What keeps me up at night are the roads we didn't take—

where an old black mustang sat empty and overgrown, the trailhead that opened
beside a decoratively overwhelmed cabin, tattered rebel flag
hoisted atop a massive front-lawn flagpole—
        things we were warned would continue
            while we still breathe
            heavy, we were warned
            that this may take every voice
                in this country, this fight—
where we arrived back at the car without having crossed a soul;
    only in retrospect have I exhaled such relief.

I go on reading, clinging to every breath and salt spilling as I find them:
couple after couple, all lesbians, murdered—off the path,
no struggle,   bound and slashed,   time and again—
        not even a trace of sexual assault: indication of a hate crime.

    Find the patterns,   the roads,   and mark them.

TINY
TOWNS

MICHAEL DOWDY

The roads end
At motels.
            —*Weldon Kees, "Travels in North America"*

Inns are not residences.
                —*Marianne Moore, "Silence"*

1.

Some folks say a family business "gets in the blood." But they're usually mum on how many generations it requires, or how many decades it takes for the blood to drain, drop by drop, as the puddle beneath your sneakers congeals into a clot of unconfirmed stories. My grandfather is a dozen years dead, my grandmother's a summer gone, my father's over seventy. Poking around their family business, I'm finding that folks also fail to add that toxins "get in the blood," too.

■ ■ ■

My family's business began with a restaurant that's eroding from my kin's memory. All that remains is a name: Tiny Town. This crack in our origin story may've been caused by a shift in our foundation, its crawl spaces now dank and impassable. For JB, my grandfather, like my father, wasn't a restaurant man. He was a motel man. The restaurants he left in a trail of ashes.

■ ■ ■

JB opened Tiny Town Restaurant in Pearisburg, near the rugged border between southwest Virginia and southern West Virginia, in 1954. Pearisburg was fifteen minutes from the shack where he was born, where three of his siblings had died, near where JB's schoolhouse burned down when he was seven, ending his formal education. I don't know why JB named the joint Tiny Town, whether it was his fondness for alliteration or a short-lived matter-of-factness. Given the man I knew and loved, it wasn't humility or any of its cousins.

■ ■ ■

Tiny Town opened when my father was five. That year he and my two uncles climbed on top of their Ripplemead trailer and threw flaming trash into my grandfather's pickup, which burned to a crisp. The temptation of fire, I'd later learn, was rumored to run in the family. Pearisburg is indeed a tiny town, but it's mammoth compared to where he grew up, between the pinpricks of Pembroke and Hoge's Chapel. The New River flows past all three dots. Unlike his aptly named restaurant, the New is a misnomer—the world's second oldest river cuts through one of the world's oldest mountain ranges. Near its banks, tiny towns like Ripplemead abound.

■ ■ ■

Another Tiny Town appears in season three of the Netflix cult classic *Arrested Development.* As the Bluth family, their family business, and the show itself unravel before our eyes, the Bluths build on the hillside behind their own model home a model-sized village of model homes. The Bluth's Tiny Town is a bait-and-switch designed to fool their Japanese investors, who will, the racist Bluths believe, stare in awe through binoculars and miss the tricks of perspective and scale. Yet it's the Bluths, not their investors, who mistake the appeal of their scheme. In their arrogance and desperation, the gigantic— their incompetence, xenophobia, and self-sabotage—shrinks. In real life, the small can appear outsized, especially up close or at high noon. Getting a durable sense of the scale and perspective of one's inheritance requires a tricky mix of curiosity and forbearance that the Bluths sorely lack.

■ ■ ■

My family's family business wasn't run by Bluthian sociopaths, and our Blue Ridge hustles were a far cry from the Bluths' Hollywood schemes. But, like theirs, ours was agonistic, dysfunctional, ever edging toward dissolution. My grandfather's Tiny Town, like many of his businesses, lasted only a few years. Like the Bluths, whose real estate acumen

consisted of hunches and gambles, JB led with his gut. Like
the Bluth patriarch George, whose Banana Stand went up
in flames, JB had a business or two burn to the ground. One
rumor ran that he torched them for insurance cash. I've found
little evidence of that, other than ashes, and ashes rarely speak.
Were his fires the result of going-it-alone? Now, cable TV
brands such instincts as DIY. Then, it was simply the ingrained
habit of scraping out of poverty. And, like George, JB was
jailed a time or two. Their "indiscretions" inscribe the shared
genetics of each family's "business." Between poker faces and
dirty laundry, boasts and shame spirals, toxic masculinities and
reparative gestures, we were made in our patriarch's images.

2.

My family called our motley rag-tag of roadside inns "the
motel business." The pronunciation of *motel* deviated from
the standard stress on the second syllable. It also departed
from the Sugarhill Gang's rendition in "Rapper's Delight," with
their equal stress on each: "HO-TELL MO-TELL, HOL-i-DAY
INNNNN." In the fashion of Appalachian vernacular English,
my folks stress the *MO*, the *tell* trapped between their lower
teeth and lips like a pinch of smokeless tobacco.

■ ■ ■

Motel is indeed distinct from *hotel*, a borrowing from
French whose first recorded use in English, according to
the *Oxford English Dictionary*, dates from 1677. A motel,
in contrast, is uniquely Unitedstatesian, the *Mo-* conjuring
motors, motion, and mobility, a history of the frontier, the
myth of progress. Symbolizing the romance of the open
road, inextricable from fishtailed cars and *Go West young
man* directives, motels are debased remainders of bourgeois

decorum and rugged masculinity alike. A hotel features elevators and interior hallways, in theory a fortress of safety. A motel's exterior doors and hallways open onto oil slicks and asphalt islands, eighteen- wheelers and Chevys. A hotel is sealed, like tempered steel. A motel is porous, like skin.

■ ■ ■

The family business started to dissolve when I was a teenager. One uncle returned to teaching, the other was retired by his sons. My cousins became teachers and social workers, faith healers and herbalists, football coaches and born agains. A couple have their own highway hotels, the family business splintered and shattered like my grandfather's ribs when he broke up a fistfight between my dad and uncle when they were nearly fifty. My dad still runs a couple, but the names no longer bear JB's imprint—no Southtowner Motel, Embassy Motor Lodge, or Huckleberry Inn—but franchise logos, respectable and dependable yet bereft of character.

■ ■ ■

The *OED* tells me that the first published instance of motel came in 1925 in the *Los Angeles Times*. "The word 'Motel,'" the report defined the term, "means motor hotels." The etymology—a compound of *motor* and *hotel*—degrades its more sophisticated French ancestor: "A roadside hotel catering primarily for motorists, typically having rooms arranged in low blocks with parking directly outside." The report then offers a mini-how-to-guide for the curious reader-traveler: "The manager of the Motel will present the driver with a key..."

■ ■ ■

This how-to guide underscores an outdated historical feature. The manager often lived inside the motel, sharing walls with guests, who could ring at any hour. My grandfather built his first live-in motel, the Imperial Motor Lodge, in 1961, in Blacksburg, Virginia, another small town where I was born fifteen years later and where I would live until I left home for good at twenty-four. When I was a toddler, my father succeeded his father as its emperor-manager. I recall it as a place for high school parties, long after my family sold it to an Indian-American family whose son was my classmate and friend. My mother remembers its old school lobby vending machine, where she gave me my first soda.

■ ■ ■

An updated how-to might warn you to watch your back, to leave no valuables in your room or car. The woman who "presents the driver with a key" may live in an exurb apartment or a trailer along an interstate access road. She's the owner's niece, picking up hours between classes at a community college. Crossing the parking lot after her shift, she may be in danger. There the desperate, weary, and addled, the precariat and sometimes homeless find themselves, sometimes with their children, sometimes with their dealer, sometimes with nausea and a dearth of pills.

■ ■ ■

Consider where my family ran motels: Bluefield, Wytheville, Elkins, Parkersburg, Galax, and Christiansburg. Places to pass through, to hole up or hide out, to catch a few hours of sleep to the humming of big rigs. Yet the motels of the fifties were built to pop, to catch the eye, not to conform to corporate specs. That's why a standard how-to-guide is of limited use: in a motel, unlike in a Hampton Inn, you don't know what you're getting. And sometimes you really don't want to know what's behind those walls.

3.

The *OED*'s entry for motel refers to a 1974 *Washington Post* article about "the oldest motel" in the U.S., which was then "alive and well" in San Luis Obispo. I like to imagine that this is the very motel Weldon Kees refers to at the start of "Travels in North America." His haunting poem was published in *Harper's* in 1952, two years before Tiny Town opened, three years before Kees disappeared in a likely suicide, and four years before the National Interstate and Defense Highways Act was passed, launching the interstate system that would transform the nation's topography. Kees's repeated "here" drops pins on a map, decades before "pin drops" entered the lexicon. "Here is San Luis Obispo," he begins. "And here, a small black dot," Kees continues,

> *Unpronounceable but hard to forget,*
> *Is where we stopped at the Seraphim Motel,*
> *And well-fed moths flew out to greet us from the walls*
> *On which a dado of petunias grew.*

The poem never lingers anywhere for long, even when the scene is alluring: "And here is Santa Barbara where / They had the heated swimming pool. / Warm in our room, we watched the bathers' breaths." None of this is celebratory, nor is it prophetic. It's simply sad. The poem deflates the allure of the open road, the freedom of the car, core American ideals underwritten by settler colonialism and Manifest Destiny. Although the poem maps the country in the early days of suburbanization and television, those totalizing pressures of Cold War conformity, the strange places Kees finds in the aggregate have a numbing effect, blending in the grey matter of a pallid Americana. So much so that "possibly the towns one never sees are best, / Preserved, remote, and merely names and distances." Pearisburg and Tiny Town could slip into his poem unnoticed, looking much the same at a Bluthian squint.

■ ■ ■

"The roads end / At motels," Kees observes, telling us one "had an Utrillo in a velvet frame." Kees doesn't say whether this was an original painting by the French modernist Maurice Utrillo, or if it was an imitation, a print, or whether it matters at all. What matters is that while the Utrillo is worthy of remark it remains unremarkable. "There seems to be no end to the motel boom," the magazine *Changing Times* declared in 1952. That end now looks nearly absolute: the motels that remain are largely trap houses, flop houses, temporary homes for the down and out, landing spots for a week or two in the absence of a social safety net. A few, like the Sunset Motel of Brevard, North Carolina, cater to nostalgia, "celebrating the best of the classic roadside motel" with "a cool kitschy retro" vibe.

■ ■ ■

The most infamous roadside motels of the fifties appear in Vladimir Nabokov's *Lolita*, published in 1955. For the novel's narrator, the pedophile Humbert Humbert, a motor lodge's appeal is two-fold: its kitsch contrasts his European sophistication, its anonymity facilitates his violence against Dolores Haze. "All along our route countless motor courts proclaimed their vacancy in neon lights," Humbert Humbert reports, "ready to accommodate salesmen, escaped convicts, impotents, family groups, as well as the most corrupt and vigorous couples." Because his sardonic tone couldn't be more different than Kees's, it baits readers into complicity. Where on this list do you place the narrator? "Ah, gentle drivers gliding through summer's black nights," Humbert Humbert wonders with mock levity, "what frolics, what twists of lust, you might see from your impeccable highways if" the motel walls "became as transparent as boxes of glass!"

■ ■ ■

Fifteen years later, Gerald Foos, he of the Nabokovian name, made Humbert Humbert's vision a reality. Decades before the reality TV shows *Big Brother* and *The Real World* scaled up voyeurism for mass consumption, Foos became the nightmare live-in manager for whom the how-to guide assumed a grotesque hue. "With the assistance of his wife," Gay Talese tells us in "The Voyeur's Motel," a *New Yorker* profile of Foos that he later adapted into a book of the same name, the couple converted the twenty-one rooms of their motel in Aurora, Colorado, into Nabokovian "boxes of glass" for what he called his "study" of sexuality. First, Foos "cut rectangular holes measuring six by fourteen inches in the ceilings." Then, "he covered the openings with louvred aluminum screens that looked like ventilation grilles but were actually observation vents that allowed him, while he knelt in the attic, to see his guests in the rooms below. He watched them for decades, while keeping an exhaustive written record of what he saw and heard. Never once, during all those years, was he caught." The chasm between "for decades" and "never once" beggars belief. Foos's elusiveness calls into question any motel's illusion of safety. It also exposes Talese, who became Foos's confessor long before he outed himself as something of an accomplice in his 2016 profile.

■ ■ ■

Foos's and my grandfather's stories converge in troubling ways. Both men named their motels in faux-Nabokovian style, in this supposedly classless country, in the manner of lords and royals. Foos: Manor House Motel. My grandfather: Imperial Motor Lodge. JB paid a fraction of the $145,000—$1.3 million in today's dollars—that Foos paid for his kingdom in 1969. So too, their towns, Aurora and Blacksburg, are coordinates on a GPS of horror. In 2012, five years after my hometown was brutalized by the mass shooting at Virginia Tech, Aurora suffered its own gun massacre, in a theater. I wish that's where their similarities ended, that my grandfather wouldn't later get caught with his pants down, another predator-king of the manor with sins to conceal.

4.

No one discusses the "incident," as I recall my family referring to it. But a backstory of predilections is emerging. One slight clue comes from 1969, when, after crossing the Georgia-Florida line, JB spotted the St. Mary's Motel side-eyeing the scruffy Sunshine State welcome center. It'd been closed for years, with many rooms converted into chicken coops. Perhaps that's why, after he bought it for a song, JB replaced the virgin's name with the humble Thrift Host Motel. But my grandfather never let humility get in the way of grandiosity.

■ ■ ■

My father has kept, like a talisman, the yellowed brochure for the Thrift Host. It highlights JB's showmanship, reminding me that he's the sole poet in my bloodline. His carnival barker's haiku asserts Guinness Book fame, hailing drivers with the freak of a motor lodge:

Thrift Host Motel
WORLD'S LONGEST MOTEL
OVER ONE-QUARTER MILE LONG!

The brochure's bird's-eye view draws my gaze not to the serpentine motel but to the Carriage Inn Restaurant and Lounge. Shaped like a cross in the foreground, it tempts the traveler with cocktails and a quick stumble beyond the shadow of the cross, where "units"—not "rooms"—promise discreet Foosian perversions. "Remember," the brochure winks, "You Get The Most With Thrift Host!" What JB meant by "most" isn't clear. What is: by that telling year, '69, and far from the tell of Tiny Town, my grandfather had developed a size fetish.

■ ■ ■

My father tells the story of a driver stopping in the parking lot as my grandfather was renovating the motel. First, he asked JB if it was open. *No*, he replied. The man peered in the distance and tried again, *What about that one down there?* Reader: it was the same motel. The brochure trumpets this length. At 1,425 feet, the drawing conjures a child's segmented toy snake hugging the woods. Undoubtedly, JB's claim to the Thrift Host's global superiority lacked an empirical study of the world's "motels," few as they were. In collapsing scales, in mistaking the nation for the world, JB's boast resembles baseball's "World" Series.

■ ■ ■

In changing the St. Mary's to the Thrift Host, JB followed his trusty taxonomy for naming properties. First, wealth worship clung like pubic hair to a bathtub's slimy grout: Royal Motor Lodge. Then, in dialectical fashion, the humble: Thrift Host Inn. Next, the grift. Holiday Lodge a hair's breadth from Holiday Inn. The corporate chain threatened a lawsuit, so JB removed his comically similar signage. The laundromat attached to one motel was named Mr. Might, a riff on Mr. Clean. Least memorable were those named after nature—Holly Inn Motel—and local gentry—the Andrew Lewis Tavern burned to a crisp when I was elementary school.

■ ■ ■

In JB's case, the outlier's telling. Grandfather's Nightclub opened in 1978 inside the Midtowner Motel in Galax, Virginia, when I was two. Grandfather's took on a mystique in my preschooler's ears. I recall the place as a source of handwringing, my reserved father flustered by the "mixed" or "rough" crowd. In my memory, Grandfather's was the scene of murders and four-alarm fires, its swinging doors regularly shuttered, my father racing in the middle of the night to defuse some situation, for when I awoke he was gone, with only the barest of euphemisms from my mother.

■ ■ ■

Why name a rowdy bar in a tough town Grandfather's? A town of shuttered furniture factories, the setting of Beth Macy's *Factory Man*, a book which caught the attention of Tom Hanks and other celebrities. Why would JB name such a place after himself, when his grandkids were toddlers, rather than resorting to his usual taxonomy? Because nothing says raucous nights and sex appeal like *grandads*? When I email him now, my father recalls Grandfather's as being beset by "encounters" between their "chief security guard" and a cast of characters he describes as "bikers with chainsaws." They went to court "a lot." Did the name provide cover?

■ ■ ■

The faded newspaper ad for the motel and restaurant is another of my father's talismans. As "Nature's Air-Conditioned City," Galax makes the Midtowner's air-conditioned "units"—not *rooms* or *suites*—redundant. The "Wall-to-Wall Carpeting" is a time capsule of the seventies. But it's the description of "Galax's Finest Restaurant" that catches my attention. Surely, a "Harness Room" and "Feed Box" promises roleplaying or S&M. I wonder now about those bikers and late night trips, about my uncle's perm and JB's weeks at a time on the road. Nah, couldn't be. Then I remember the joint's mechanical bull. Cosplay it was, the charm of the Old West manifest even there in that "air-conditioned" Appalachian city.

■ ■ ■

My grandfather's roads ended at motels like the Thrift Host and the Midtowner. Some years, he clocked 80,000 miles in his El Camino, prowling U.S. 1 or winding up switchbacks into West Virginia. Cash poor, he'd saunter into a rambling roadside motel, tucked under a slagged bank or a scamper across a weedy parking lot from a diner. Word was he bought two on handshakes. Then came the crash, near Galax, that whipped him, seatbelt stiff against the door, through the windshield and into the interstate's riverine ditch. Peripheral vision gone, never to drive again, his roads were barricaded with all but one secret deadbolted behind his carpeted "units."

5.

My grandfather, then my father, ran motels. I've been running toward a dark room of false walls, chasing the echoes of predator-emperors like Foos and, I fear, my grandfather. When I was fifteen, on Columbus Day weekend, my father bolted to bail him out of jail somewhere up the West Virginia Turnpike. I don't recall the threadbare story precisely, and my father remains silent. But it's a common, contemptuous tale. Office tryst gone too far. Disgruntled employee. Baseless accusations. Out for money. I'm tempted to say, *Well, who knows really?* But when the truth hits below the belt, I want blood. My blood. My childhood idol's "good name." After the rape charge was dropped by the grand jury, the family never mentioned it again. I am the grandson of a "good man" accused of rape. Like most white men, I am the ancestor of such Columbuses. Their sins, half-shriven and half-forgotten, buried in our dampest crawl spaces.

■ ■ ■

After his traumatic injury, JB became a thorn in the side of the family business. He insisted on new marquees for their few motels. Sometimes his mocked-up signs announced VETERAN OWNED, at others AMERICAN OWNED. Many motels then and now are owned by Indian-Americans, by families whose surnames are Singh and Patel and Sanghani. Were my brain-sick grandfather's signs euphemisms for *White Owned*? Did they invert Jim Crow's *Whites Only* signs, concerned not with the customer's race but with the owner's?

Perhaps he saw the new generation of Indian motel men as competitors and was seeking an advantage, one that ran skin-deep and was lanced with irony. My grandfather's mother was Cherokee. His skin was leathery and dark as a catcher's mitt. No, his brain, like his country's, was hotwired for bigotry.

■ ■ ■

The Thrift Host's brochure ends with an exuberant couplet inviting "the discriminating motoring public" to "Please travel safely on your way. / And please come back another day!" This earnestness characterized the manic, repetitive letters my grandfather wrote me on yellow legal pads after his accident, during my first year away at college. Although I cherished those notes and keep them still as amulets against forgetting, back then, as I grew mountainsick in the Tidewater, I needed a more roughshod and resilient language to explain myself to myself. Before I slipped into the tailspin that sent Kees, at the end of his travels, off a bridge and into a river.

■ ■ ■

My grandfather's unraveling, amplified by his exile from his car, coincided with my splitting apart, with debilitating panic attacks and a mortifying ER trip. Should I join my family's motel men shuttling between "the towns one never sees" and non-places like Yulee, site of the world's longest motor lodge? Or, should I follow my nose into the books I was discovering at my 300 year-old college named for a king and a queen? I quit school, went home, and told myself I could see the world by reading. Within two years, I realized, as *Arrested Development*'s heedless Gob Bluth often says, *I've made a huge mistake*. The road's call courses in my blood, a disquiet that skipped my father, a restlessness like JB's that pricks the throat as much as the foot on the gas.

■ ■ ■

My father, who rarely dispenses unsolicited advice, always warned me: *Never get in the restaurant business.* The late hours, the unreliable "help," the slim margins, the competition. He's never uttered a single admonition about the "motel business." Did he assume it rustled my blood and lifted my tongue, a strong beat that, once voiced, couldn't be unstressed? He still tells me, after fifteen years as a professor, that I'm welcome back in the business. I don't tell him that my road began at motels, that his ends were my beginnings. I don't say that the business, like our words and bodies, isn't built to last. I simply passed through it, but only after, in my great fortune, he gave me a stable starting position. The family business's privilege and isolation alike are only "mine" here inside my sentences, the units of my story.

■ ■ ■

"Hospitality," the French Algerian theorist Jacques Derrida wrote, "carries within it the concept of hostility." *Host, guest, hospitality*, and *hostile* share an etymology, blurring the supposedly bright line between welcome and menace. Searching for clues that make bedfellows of *hospitality* and *hostility*, I imagine walking into the padlocked office of my family's old Parkersburg motel, where the assault did or did not happen. As the key rusts in the bottom drawer of my father's memory, my search of the available public records keeps coming up empty. Only questions remain. Is the cost of throwing your ancestors under the bus greater than the price of protecting their stories? Does papering over the false wall between past and present tilt the scales of guilt and exoneration? Who has the will and the way to see through walls? Who's trapped, unwittingly, behind them? For whom is the air-conditioned room a refuge? For whom is wall-to-wall-carpeting a scene of entrapment, cigarette burns and sketchy needles? Where does the motor lodge's residence in the landscape of the American imaginary linger? How many generations must batter the locked doors of patriarchy's secretive lairs before the hinges buckle and snap?

■ ■ ■

I come from a family whose Tiny Town perched above a very old river called the New, a world of small and smaller towns nestled in low and disappearing mountains. I dreamt of leaving, then I dreamt of coming back. After I left for good I mostly stopped dreaming, though the mountains still shadow nearly every sentence I write. I'm not a motel man like my father and grandfather before him. I'm good with that. That I'm no longer a mountain man is another story. The mountains get in the blood unlike any business or family tradition or any toxin like money or masculinity. After all, at two hundred million years old, they're my oldest living relations. ■

FIRST FROST

The snow line on the mountain
is crisp and white, easing down
to swallow autumn like a ripe apple.

One day we wake to find
the yard full of deer, antlers
pointing every direction. A pair
searching for warmth in the glaze
of once-sweet grass.

It has been a long time since
a doe appeared this close. I think
they must be hungry now.
Or, how nothing we know
really ever leaves us.

KATY LUXEM

DAYLIGHT SAVINGS

When pulling the dead flowers free, I stopped time
for a moment to notice the losing sunlight. Loose dirt
shook off like the hours of the day. The darkness
came early, shaded by the mountain so there was no
edge to it. I dragged the bodies away. I didn't
notice the seeds scatter like migrating birds headed to the
warm center of our earth. May they wait the long winter
for a precarious spring. May I forget them in the night,
as a dream flies elsewhere. Until the sun rises early,
a marigold waiting for me on the other side.

KATY LUXEM

BOOK REVIEWS

Tiffany McDaniel. *Betty: A Novel.* **New York, N.Y.: Alfred A. Knopf, 2020. 480 pages. Hardcover. $26.95.**

Reviewed by Hannah D. Markley

"This book is part dance, part song, and part shine of the moon," McDaniel writes on the dedication page to her mother, Betty, namesake and inspiration for a novel whose narrative dances with multiple histories—familial, cultural, and regional, sings with lyrical prose, and moves through the woods of a young woman's life, partially illuminating the traumas and their impact therein.

Betty spins out from the Carpenter family's origin—her parents coupling in a cemetery in Appalachian Ohio. Betty Carpenter is a middle child of eight children, and after a quick marriage, the family wanders around the country for several years before heading back home to Breathed, Ohio. McDaniel writes, "In her most wholesome form, Breathed was a wife and mother who made sure to hang her flag banners on her porch rails every Fourth of July. At her darkest, she was the place you could bleed to death without a single open wound." This dance between caretaker and wound plays out not only in Breathed, but also in the family drama. The hills, creeks, flora, and fauna of rural Ohio become a complicated ally and accomplice in the family's woes. Her father makes a living off the land, and yet is never fully accepted by the town of Breathed because of his Cherokee heritage. The Carpenters are a winding, twisting world with strong yet uncertain ties to one another, the love tangled in with the pain.

Betty's voice narrates these many layers of history with a consistent, precise voice. However, at times, the speed of the plot moves at such a pace that their intertwining stories seem beyond the author's grasp. Because of the breadth of characters and pace of the plot, key characters—most notably Betty's mother, Alka—lack the space to develop complexity on the page, leaving them partially realized.

But McDaniel's lyrical prose sings through every chapter of the book. Describing the Carpenters early on, she writes, "When I think of my family now, I think of a big ol' sorghum field, like the one my father was born in. Dry brown dirt, wet green leaves. A mad sweetness there in the hard canes. That's my family. Milk and honey and all that old-time bullshit." Like this one, images in *Betty* announce themselves with vivacity. The words crunch and slip, strumming the dips and rises of backwoods Ohio. The images, though gritty in many scenes, contain grace notes that add delicacy and humanity to the trauma. In one of the first chapters McDaniel shares one such embellishment when Landon Carpenter, Betty's father, goes to pick up Alka from her parents' home, a rescue mission of sorts considering Alka's father, Grandpappy Lark, has already hit Alka to the ground for her growing pregnant belly. In the moment of Landon's arrival, Alka is packing up her belongings, "'What am I forgettin'?' She looked around the room. ...[S]he looked at the short cotton curtains framing the window. The curtains were yellow and had little white flowers printed on them. She wondered if she needed such prettiness to dress up the place she was going, wherever that might be. 'Yes,' she answered herself." This is the prettiness, too, that McDaniel's language intones. Outside that window, Landon is punching her father in the dirt, and she's giving the reader a tinge of hope in the landscape never far from the next trouble.

Even though cotton curtains flutter and moonshine spills onto the hills, *Betty* contains profoundly dark moments. As a preteen, Betty uncovers and then buries the stories she sees hurting her family, "*Try again. Breathe. Write these words faster. Those ones slower. Look at the dish towels drying on the porch rail. Stories hide in the usual places...* I dropped the pieces into a glass jar full of half-drunk moonshine there on the table. I watched the liquor bleed the ink away, and sat there long enough that the shadows shifted in the lowering sun."

Themes of incest, violence, self-harm, and racism appear throughout the book, with some scenes more explicit than others. Though McDaniel renders painful moments with economy and vividness, some of these scenes appear somewhat detached and underdeveloped within the characters and plot. At times, the older, reflective version of Betty seems to be present to the darkness within the scene, guiding the reader through with certainty, but at other times she hides within the younger Betty, leaving the reader to sort through the impact of the trauma for herself.

No family's story is simple. *Betty* is a novel all at once admirable in scope and unsettling in content, and, though the book realizes an intricate dance as it combines layers of history with lyrical language and images, it never fully finds the heartbeat of the complex trauma in the fictional Carpenter family. While this aspect of the novel misses a few steps, a reader looking for a complex cast of characters or a plot concerned with a coming-of-age story about a young, Cherokee-Appalachian woman, will find in *Betty* a worthwhile, challenging, and absorbing read. ∎

Yaa Gyasi. *Transcendent Kingdom*. New York, N.Y.: Alfred A. Knopf, 2020. 288 pages. Hardcover. $27.95.

Reviewed by Margaret Ann Snow

In *Transcendent Kingdom*, Yaa Gyasi writes of pain and loss so vividly the reader feels it, as if they are actually experiencing it themselves. Gifty, the narrator, is conducting research on mice as a PhD candidate in neuroscience while also tending to and worrying about her depressed mother who rarely gets out of bed. Stories from Gifty's past are interspersed with moments from the present day. The scenes from her past are not in chronological order. Instead, they are more thoughtfully given to readers to keep us wanting more. Her story begins before she was born, when her mother and father meet in Ghana.

Gifty's father is only ever referred to as the *Chin Chin Man*, a name he earned for the deep-fried snacks made of flour, sugar, milk, and butter that he convinced Gifty's Ghanian grandmother to give him for free. However, Gifty's mother's name is never mentioned. In journaling to God, Gifty refers to her as *The Black Mamba*. Her parents are married in Ghana, and her older brother, Nana, is born there. Her mother wants to give her new baby everything and decides moving to America is the way to do so, a decision Gifty eventually questions: "this place was everything [her] mother hoped for that day when she asked God where she should go to give her son the world."

While her father is never keen on moving to America, he quickly follows his wife and young son, but longs for Ghana. In America, he is accused of stealing in Walmart "three times in four months…Homesick, humiliated, he stopped leaving the house." Eventually, he returns to Ghana, where he feels free to be a strong, proud, Black man. The *Chin Chin Man*'s absence from his family reverberates throughout the story and leaves Gifty's mother a single, working parent in a foreign country.

There are occasions of racism throughout the novel and Gifty's childhood. In the Sunday School room at her church, Gifty overhears two women talking about her brother Nana, a gifted basketball player who has transformed the local team. But Nana is battling an injury, and his doctor, who wants to see him back on the court, has prescribed Oxycontin. "Their kind does seem to have a taste for drugs," the women whisper. Afterwards, Gifty's names feelings of internalized racism before there was a term for it: "I grew up only with my part, my little throbbing stone of self-hate that I carried around with me to church, to school, to all those places in my life that worked, it seemed to me then, to affirm the idea that I was irreparably, fatally, wrong." The drug quickly consumes Nana, filling a void created by the emptiness left by his father, his own internalized racism, or any number of other reasons, and it leads him to other drugs. After Nana is pressed on what it feels like when he takes the drugs, he answers, "like everything inside my head just empties out and then there is nothing left—in a good way."

Gyasi forces readers to see addicts beyond their addiction and the depressed beyond their depression—to face our own participation in the stigma that prevents these people from receiving the care and help they need. In a park, Gifty holds Nana's feet, and their mother holds his upper body. They carry him, passed out, to the car. Remembering this day, she says, "The thing I will never forget is that people were watching us do all of this[...]and no one lifted a finger."

After years of trying to fight addiction and eventually learning to coexist with it, police tell Gifty and her mother that Nana has overdosed on heroin in a Starbucks parking lot and is dead. Gifty's doctoral research on reward-seeking behavior in mice is directly related to losing her brother. She chooses this research as a way to "work through all of [her] misunderstandings about his addiction and all [her] shame." Through the research, she hopes to find answers to her questions: "Why didn't Nana stop? Why didn't he get better for us? For me?"

Transcendent Kingdom also tackles the division between science and religion. As a young girl, Gifty believes in God with her whole being. She journals to him as her form of prayer. She and her mother attend church every Sunday. This belief wavers as her life unfolds and reveals itself in all its disappointment and pain. Religion comes up in a small group during a college science course. When she asks the group how they know God does not exist, they look at her like she is crazy. After that, she thinks they see her as "[a] backwoods bama, a Bible thumper." The question of whether one can believe in science and also in God runs through the book as Gifty works through it in her mind.

The end finds her on a drive with no destination. She pulls over, sits in her car pleading, or maybe finding a new form of prayer. The last pages feel abrupt, possibly because it doesn't provide the closure the reader craves, or because we want more of Gifty's stories—more about her mother, more of the complex relationship between mother and daughter, or simply more of Yaa Gyasi's words. ■

TURNING THE DOGS

In boxes they cry out.
Bellows ring through the tatter
of tails against black bars
and nails claw liner
from a steel pickup bed.
Latches and locks drop
a muffled stampede
of paws to the ground.
Hear the scratch of broom
sage bowed to their bellies
and briar-beat teats,
cracked from this year's
litter. In cotton pockets
their masters fumble shells,
shuffle boots in the frost
and mud, kick up the breath
of morning as it rises
in a purple sun,
bruised with opening day.
That invisible welling
rustled in the dead leaves'
crunch, taste of rabbit
rolled back and chambered
in their throats. First
yelps sound—cut tracks—
and round the pack
back to the bend where
hunters howl and shed
their shape of men.

ADAM MOORE

CONTRIBUTORS

Jaycee Billington is from Folkston, Georgia and received her MFA from the Iowa Writers' Workshop. Her work appears in *Plain China, the peacock's feet, Hotel Amerika, Bread and Assembly, West Trade Review*, and *The Oyez Review*. She is the winner of a Wilson Award for excellence in writing.

Originally from Country Kildare in Ireland, **Gavin Colton** lives and works in Lexington, Kentucky. He holds an MFA from The University of Kentucky. His words have appeared in *Hippocampus, The Wax Paper, La Picoletta Barca, Loch Norse Magazine, MHK Magazine, The Manifest-Station*, and *The Kentucky Kernel*.

Michael Dowdy is a poet, critic, essayist, and editor. His books include a collection of poems, *Urbilly* (Main Street Rag Poetry Book Award, 2017); a study of Latinx poetry, *Broken Souths: Latina/o Poetic Responses to Neoliberalism and Globalization* (University of Arizona Press, 2013); and, as coeditor with Claudia Rankine, a critical anthology, *American Poets in the 21st Century: Poetics of Social Engagement* (Wesleyan University Press, 2018). He teaches at the University of South Carolina.

Ace Englehart is a Richmond, Virginia native and recent MFA graduate in Poetry from the University of Tennessee, Knoxville with a BA in English from Virginia Commonwealth University. Her work has been featured in online magazines *Unlimited Literature, Persephone's Daughters, A Murder of Storytellers*, and VCU's *Poictesme* (pwa-tem). Ace enjoys photography, karaoke, camping and swimming, as well as spending time at home with her partner Holly and their three pets.

David S. Higdon is a writer from Kentucky. His work has been published or is forthcoming in *Still: The Journal, Rust + Moth, Exposition Review, Lucky Jefferson, Coffin Bell Journal*, and others. He is the 2021 winner of The Grand Prix Prize from the Kentucky State Poetry Society. He lives with his family in Louisville.

Jason Kyle Howard is the author of *A Few Honest Words* and *Something's Rising* (with Silas House). His work has appeared in numerous publications including the *New York Times, Oxford American, Salon, The Nation, The Millions, Utne Reader, Paste,* and *Sojourners.* He is editor of *Appalachian Review,* a literary quarterly based at Berea College, where he also teaches and directs the creative writing program. He serves on the faculty of the Spalding University Naslund-Mann Graduate School of Writing in Louisville.

Originally from North Carolina, **Christopher Labaza** is an undergraduate studying creative writing and music at Emory University in Atlanta, Georgia. At Emory, he was awarded the Grace Abernethy Scholarship for his fiction. He is currently working on a short story collection about life in the South.

Rebecca Lilly has earned degrees from Cornell (MFA) and Princeton (PhD) Universities and works as a writer and photographer. Among her several collections of poems, her most recent is *Creatures Among Us* (Broadstone, 2019). An earlier collection, *You Want to Sell Me a Small Antique* (Gibbs Smith), won the Peregrine Smith Poetry Prize, and several books of her short poetry and haiku appear from Red Moon Press. Her website is RebeccaLilly.studio.

Katy Luxem (she/her) grew up in Seattle and studied creative writing at the University of Washington. Her work has appeared or is forthcoming in *Rattle, The National Poetry Review, North Dakota Quarterly, McSweeney's Internet Tendency,* and *The Mum Poem Press* edited by Liz Berry, among others. She lives in Salt Lake City with her partner, kids, and dogs.

Hannah D. Markley is a freelance writer and educator. She lives in central Kentucky and is in the creative writing MFA program at Pacific Lutheran University where she is also on the editorial staff for *Soundings,* the program's online publication. Her writing appears in *Bitter Southerner.*

Originally from central Mississippi, **Adam Moore** is a PhD (Poetry) student at the Center for Writers at the University of Southern Mississippi. His recent work appears or is forthcoming in *Valley Voices* and *New Limestone Review.*

Jeremy Paden was raised in Nicaragua, Costa Rica, and the Dominican Republic. He is a poet, translator, and professor of Latin American literature at Transylvania University in Lexington, Kentucky. He is the author of four collections of poems. Among these, *ruina montium*, about the 2010 Chilean mine collapse, has been published in both English (Broadstone Books, 2016) and Spanish (Valparaíso, 2018). He is also the translator for various poets from Argentina, Chile, Colombia, and Spain.

Jacquelyn Scott has an MFA from The University of Tennessee. Her work has appeared or is forthcoming in *The Laurel Review, The Blue Mountain Review, December Mag*, and elsewhere. Find her on a hiking trail or on Twitter @JacquelynLScott.

Margaret Ann Snow lives in Tuscaloosa, Alabama, where she spends her days farming, mothering, reading and writing. In 2004, along with her partner and husband David, she started Snow's Bend Farm. Both her farm work and her writing are inspired by a love of good food, a conviction to care for the land and people, the scientific aspects of farming, a passion for plants, and a wonderment of nature.

www.ingramcontent.com/pod-product-compliance
Lightning Source LLC
Chambersburg PA
CBHW070603180626
46817CB00005B/1967